T0101394

5-MINUTE
DEVOTIONS
for girls

To: . . . .

From: . . . .

Date: . . . .

5-MINUTE
DEVOTIONS
for girls

faithgirlz

5-MINUTE
DEVOTIONS
for girls

Featuring

~~~ **180** ~~~

DAILY DEVOTIONS

ZONDERkidz™

ZONDERKIDZ

5-Minute Devotions for Girls
Copyright © 2019 by Zondervan

Requests for information should be addressed to:
Zondervan, *3900 Sparks Dr. SE, Grand Rapids, Michigan 49546*

Library of Congress Cataloging-in-Publication Data

Names: Smith, Laura L., 1969- author.
Title: 5-minute devotions for girls / Laura L. Smith.
Other titles: Five-minute devotions for girls
Description: Grand Rapids, Michigan : Zonderkidz, [2020] | Series:
    Faithgirlz | Audience: Ages: 8-12. |
Identifiers: LCCN 2018047885 (print) | LCCN 2019000058 (ebook) |
    ISBN 9780310763130 () | ISBN 9780310763123 (hardcover)
Subjects: LCSH: Girls—Prayers and devotions—Juvenile literature. |
    Bible--Quotations—Juvenile literature.
Classification: LCC BV4860 (ebook) | LCC BV4860 .S65 2020 (print) |
    DDC 242/.62—dc23
LC record available at https://lccn.loc.gov/2018047885

Content by: Laura L. Smith
Interior design: Denise Froehlich

Printed in the United States of America

---

20 21 22 23 24 /LSC/ 10 9 8 7 6 5 4 3 2

Introduction

He asked the best questions and was an amazing listener. He treated us like what was going on in our lives was important. Because it was. I'm certain this is why Mr. Cook is the one Sunday school teacher I remember. I remember his name, face, and voice, but mainly how he treated all the students gathered around in plastic chairs like they were his equals.

Mr. Cook was also the first person who challenged me to get to know my Bible. He taught me how the Bible pertained to the ups, downs, triumphs, and challenges of my daily life. I still have a verse card he gave me. On one side it listed emotions—when you're nervous, when you're excited, when you're angry, etc. On the other side were a handful of Bible verses that applied to those life situations. It opened my eyes. The Bible wasn't just for church or for learning about God, although it was good for both of those things, but it was also for understanding how personally God loved *me*—how he was always there for me, no matter what was going on.

I want this devotional to be everything that Mr. Cook was for me and more. The things you are going through do matter. These years are great years, important years . . . but also challenging years in your life—you'll have friends, frenemies, and the kid who always finds something to pick on you about. You'll laugh and argue with your parents. You'll play and fight with your siblings. You'll try to do the right things. Sometimes you'll mess up. You'll have tryouts and award ceremonies. Sometimes you'll make the team and earn the star and other times you won't. But God's Word, the Bible, has the absolute best advice for *all* those situations. It's not just for church days. Because every day, no matter what you're experiencing, no matter if you've slipped up or achieved great things, God thinks you're awesome and loves you deeply. God will give you everything you need to move forward and to stand tall. The Bible is your handbook to help figure all that stuff out.

I praise you because I am fearfully and wonderfully made.

−Psalm 139:14

For I know the plans I have for you," declares the LORD, "plans to prosper you and not to harm you, plans to give you hope and a future.

−Jeremiah 29:11

It's been a while since I sat in Mr. Cook's classroom, but now I have four kids of my own. I cheer in their triumphs and hold them during their struggles. I hear their laughter and wipe their tears. The main thing I want my kids to know is how much Jesus truly loves them. I wish I could look you in your eyes and tell you how much Jesus loves you, how amazing He thinks you are. But since I can't tell you face-to-face, I wrote this devotional to remind you each day how God designed you to be amazing, and that when you turn to Him, He will help you be your true, beautiful, incredible self.

For you created my inmost being; you knit me together in my mother's womb. I praise you because I am fearfully and wonderfully made.
—Psalm 139:13-14

Who are you? Are you artsy? Athletic? Preppy? Funky? Are you loud or quiet? Do you like to read or run or ride horses? Are you tall or short? Do you have a houseful of siblings or are you an only child? Is math your favorite subject or is it recess? No matter what you like or how you look, you are made wonderfully by God. And that word "fearfully" doesn't mean "scary," it means, "to inspire awe," as in *awesome.*

Let that sink in for a minute. God, the creator of the universe, the one who's in charge of everything, he knitted you together stitch by stitch before you were even born. That means you are incredibly valuable. And all those special things about you—the shape of your nose, the color of your hair, the things that make your brain tick and your heart smile—God put all that stuff into you, and he did it on purpose. So know that whatever your interests are, whatever you look like, God made you and he made you wonderful and awesome.

What makes you special and unique? What are the things you love to do? The things that make you smile? Grab a piece of paper and sketch a picture of yourself, thanking God for making you exactly who you are. Write the words "wonderful" and "awesome" somewhere on your picture to remind yourself how God created you.

You are to be holy to me because I, the LORD, am holy, and I have set you apart from the nations to be my own.

–Leviticus 20:26

Sometimes you won't get picked. You won't get selected for the team. You won't be put in the advanced class. You won't get a part in the play. You won't get called on even though your hand is raised high. You won't get invited to the party.

It happens to all of us. And it hurts. But God does pick you. Always. God calls you to be his daughter. He chooses you to love. He sets you apart, and not off to the side somewhere, but to be his very own. Just like you might pick out a puppy that warms your heart. No matter who else does or doesn't choose you, God chooses you every day. He chooses you every time. He loves you for who you are. He sees you and he wants you on his team, he sets you in the highest places, he gives you the leading role, he wants to hear what you have to say, and he invites you to be with him always.

Think of something you hope you get chosen for (captain of your team, your painting in the art show, etc.). Let God know what you're hoping for, but also thank him for already choosing you to be his blessed daughter. Ask God to remind you how special you are to him whether you get chosen or not.

"For where two or three gather in my name, there am I with them."

—Matthew 18:20

Ever have a hard time making the right choices, choosing to live how God wants you to? When your classmates talk about how weird the substitute teacher is, it's hard *not* to chime in. When your friends want to watch a movie your parents don't want you to watch, it's tricky to say, "Let's watch something else." But if you have friends who also love Jesus, who also want to honor God with their actions, it gets a lot easier. Together, you and your friend can say something nice about the sub or change the subject when friends talk badly about her. When you suggest a different movie, your friend can back you up. This doesn't mean God isn't with you when you're alone. He is. God's with you always, but he still gives us Christian friends to help us stay close to him.

Don't have any friends like this? Pay attention. I bet you'll notice some kids on your team or in your class who choose good words and good works. Get to know them. Life's easier when you have someone who stands up for what you believe in with you.

Name a friend who helps you stay close to God. If you don't have friends like this, list some people you think might know God, some kids who you've noticed make good decisions. Say a prayer thanking God for your Christian friends or asking him to help you find some. Then ask God to help you stand strong together.

4

But those who hope in the LORD will renew their strength. They will soar on wings like eagles; they will run and not grow weary, they will walk and not be faint.

–Isaiah 40:31

Some days you'll feel exhausted. It could be because you stayed up doing homework, you had a late game or practice, you had a lot on your mind and couldn't fall asleep, you're run down or not feeling well, or maybe all of the above have happened several days in a row. Whew! It's hard to concentrate and keep going when you feel like this. Of course the best thing to do when you're tired is to try to get some sleep. But it's also important to remember that God promises to renew you—just like a good nap.

If you put your hope in God, he will help you soar during the important times, even when you feel like you can barely crawl. That doesn't mean you won't ever feel sleepy or that you should stay up super late. It means when you trust in God he will give you extra energy you didn't have on your own, to do the things he calls you to do.

If your bedtime's been late, try to figure out how to get to bed earlier this week. Then ask God to give you the energy you need to do the important stuff. Write out today's verse and put it somewhere you'll see in the morning, like on the bathroom mirror, to remind you that God will energize you each day.

For God so loved the world that he gave his one and only Son, that whoever believes in him shall not perish but have eternal life.

—John 3:16

God loves you. He does. Even when it feels like no one understands you, like no one else loves you, like God is a million miles away. He loves you.

How can you know for sure? Because he sent his son, Jesus, down to earth to become a person, so he would know exactly what it feels like to be stressed, excited, hurt, happy, sad, nervous, even hungry and tired. That way he can help you when you're feeling any of those things, because he knows how you feel. God wanted to understand everything about you. You're that important to God!

And then God allowed his perfect son to die on the cross and take all the punishment for anything wrong you've ever done or ever will do, so that you could be free and forgiven. Wow! Not because you did something amazing, but because God would do anything for you, give up anything for you, even die for you. So, if you're wondering, know down to your center that God loves you. He wants only the best for you. And God would do anything; in fact, he did *everything*, so that he and you can be together forever.

Think of someone you love. It could be your dog or a friend or one of your parents. Would you give up everything for them? God did exactly that for you. Thank God for giving up the thing that was most precious to him for you, for loving you that much.

6

And we know that in all things God works for the good of those who love him, who have been called according to his purpose.

—Romans 8:28

What's going on with you today? Are you happy? Sad? Excited about something that might happen? Confused about something that did or didn't happen? Every day seems like it's full of things to look forward to and things you might be uncertain about. Whatever you're up to today—headed to school, practice, a competition, doing chores, whatever it is— God is working in and through these things.

Homework seems boring? God could be using the very thing you're learning today in science class to help you discover a new planet or to find a cure for a disease one day. Did your game get rained out? Maybe God knows how much you need some rest, and since you can't go to your game, you can go to bed early. Hesitant to go to the youth cookout? Somebody else who's coming might be your future best friend. Whatever is going on in your life, good or bad, God will use it for good.

~~~~~~~~~~~~~~~~~~

God already knows everything that's going on with you, but he loves it when you talk to him about it. Close your eyes and tell him something that's worrying or concerning you, something you don't understand. Ask God to help you through this challenging time, while he's using it for something good.

You alone are the LORD. You made the heavens, even the highest heavens, and all their starry host, the earth and all that is in it, the seas and all that is in them. You give life to everything, and the multitudes of heaven worship you.

–Nehemiah 9:6

The closest star to earth is the sun. It's 93 million miles away. The next closest stars (Alpha Centauri A and B) are 4.35 light years away from us. And yet, the entire sky is dotted with the bright, beautiful lights of stars that God created.

The oceans cover more than 70 percent of the earth! All that salt water would fill 352,670,000,000,000,000,000 gallon-sized milk containers, and God made every drop of it.

God made every tree and animal and lake and mountain. He made every living thing, even you. It's hard to get our brains around how amazing God is, how all-encompassing he is. But he is huger than huge, bigger than big, phenomenally phenomenal! He created everything—not just everything we can see, but everything that has been created. If God can create all the stars and planets, including earth, its oceans, and everything on it—he can do anything. He is a God worth praising.

What are your favorite things in nature? Write them down. Do you love climbing trees? Write words in the branches and leaves. Are you a beach girl who can play in the waves all day? List sand, surf, and sun. Write, "Thank you, God!" or, "You are incredible, God!" next to each item on your list.

I will give you a new heart and put a new spirit in you; I will remove from you your heart of stone and give you a heart of flesh.

—Ezekiel 36:26

Ever said something nasty and wished you could take it back? Ever told your parents that you made your bed, practiced your piano, or brushed your teeth, even though you hadn't . . . yet? Ever been jealous of someone else's shoes or how late they can stay up? Ever lost your temper? Stomped out of the room? Slammed a door? Pushed someone or their bag or their books on purpose?

We are human. And we do mess up. Thankfully, Jesus doesn't expect us to be perfect. In fact, he loves us exactly as we are, exactly as he made us to be. That's why God is always there for us, always guiding us, helping us to learn from our mistakes, giving us patience to not get so frustrated, peace to not get angry, joy in what we have, so we don't wish for what we don't have. If we ask him for help, God will take out the bad stuff that bogs down our thoughts and actions and replace it with a more caring, loving heart.

This is the perfect time to hand over to God any time or way you've messed up. Tell him how you feel. Ask God for forgiveness. Ask him to help you do better next time, to change your heart. Then take a deep breath, a sigh of relief, knowing you have been completely forgiven—that God is on your side.

Have I not commanded you? Be strong and courageous. Do not be afraid; do not be discouraged, for the LORD your God will be with you wherever you go.

—Joshua 1:9

Are you afraid of the dark, of being alone, of spiders or mice? There might be a person who intimidates you—a principal, a coach, a bully. Sometimes it's a certain place or incident that's frightening, like going to the dentist or standing up in front of a group. In *The Wizard of Oz*, the Cowardly Lion was afraid of everything! In fact, he was so scared all the time, all he wanted was courage, and he would do anything to get some. But we don't have to fight off flying monkeys or even follow the yellow brick road to get courage.

God tells us he'll be with us wherever we go, in every situation. He says there's nothing to be afraid of, because he's right there by our side. That means God's there in the dark uncertain places, holding your hand. It means he'll stand beside you when the person who frightens you gives you a hard time. It means he'll hold you when your knees knock or when your hands shake. God doesn't give you a gold badge to pin to your shirt, but he gives you something better—strength, courage, and love in everything you're facing.

Make a list of all the things you're afraid of. It doesn't matter if they're truly terrifying or if it's something silly—like clowns—write them down. Then take a big black marker and write over the entire list, "DO NOT BE AFRAID! GOD IS WITH ME!"

Because of the LORD's great love we are not consumed, for his compassions never fail. They are new every morning; great is your faithfulness.

–Lamentations 3:22-23

Good morning, sunshine! It's a brand-new day full of possibilities and potential. The sun is in the sky and your lungs are breathing in fresh air. Wherever you're going today is a chance to chat with a friend or meet a new one, an opportunity to make someone smile, a spot where you might learn something new. Whatever happened yesterday is over. Don't let the stress from last night's homework or missing the shot at practice overwhelm you today. You can learn from it. You can grow from it. But you have to move on from it.

So what would you like to do today? Bring up your grade in math? Go for a bike ride? Work on your dribbling? Bake cookies? Write a note to your grandma? God is with you on this day, loving you and cheering for you in all that you're experiencing. God is excited to see what adventures you'll go on and how you'll live this amazing gift of twenty-four hours to its fullest.

If you could do anything today, what would it be? What's something you've been meaning to do, but haven't gotten around to? Ask God what he thinks is the best use of your time today. Praise him for the opportunities that await you and seize them when they come your way.

You make known to me the path of life; you will fill me with joy in your presence, with eternal pleasures at your right hand.

—Psalm 16:11

Isn't it fun to get a new pair of shoes or headband? Do you keep looking in the mirror or down at your feet, touching your headband, or bouncing in your shoes? God loves to fill you with happiness that will last forever—way longer than your shoes or headbands.

God is constantly making new paths where there weren't any before. That means if you like to hike, you might find a new trail, or if you're struggling to find things to eat with your food allergy, your mom might make something new for dinner that you discover is delicious. It could mean you're going to learn a different way of playing guitar that's easier for you. It means if you feel like you're stuck, or there's no way out of your current situation, God is busy inventing ladders and secret tunnels so you can get to all the great things he has in store for you. As fun as it is to get something new, God loves to surprise you with the happy feeling you get when you're with him even more. Are you ready for him to fill you with joy?

~~~~~~~~~~~~~~~~~

What are you wishing was different? Where do you feel stuck today? Close your eyes and ask God to show you a new path. After you ask, keep your eyes closed. Stay silent. Focus on God creating new options and opportunities for you. When you open your eyes, keep them open for his surprises.

When the angel of the LORD appeared to Gideon, he said, "The LORD is with you, mighty warrior."

–Judges 6:12

Who do you think of when you hear "mighty warrior?" Susan in Narnia shooting her bow and arrow? Rosa Parks for for not giving up her seat on the bus? I want to tell you a secret. It's also you. Yes, *you* are a mighty warrior! You may not have a sword and a shield or a lightsaber, but you have something way more powerful. You have God.

What battles are you fighting today? Is there a kid who gets picked on at lunch? You are a mighty warrior. That means you can stand up *to* the bully, stand up *for* that person. Is there a girl on your team who's always last when you're running laps? You are a mighty warrior. You can drop back and run alongside her, just like a hero would go back in the fire to save someone in a burning house. Is there something you're fighting—a cold, depression, asthma—something that makes you feel weak, like maybe you just can't do it today? You are a mighty warrior! God has empowered you to fight your battles and he's got your back every step of the way.

Draw a picture of yourself as a mighty warrior—whatever that means to you. Give yourself the "armor" or "weapons" to fight your personal battles. And then draw God next to you, even more powerful than you. Whisper a prayer asking him for strength in all your battles today.

> For we are God's handiwork, created in Christ
> Jesus to do good works, which God prepared in
> advance for us to do.
>
> *–Ephesians 2:10*

What do you like to make? Do you enjoy fixing snacks or baking treats? Are you handy, carving things out of wood? Or techy, able to design gorgeous graphics or code perfect software commands? Maybe you're crafty—beading bracelets or painting canvases?

Think of the things you make, how much effort and care you put into them, how much time you spend making them, how good you feel when you've completed your creation. That's how God feels about you. You are his handiwork. Not his sketch or doodle, but the thing he spent time on, the thing he took special care creating. Do you love swirling the frosting just so on a cupcake or planning out the colors for a painting? Do you use special tools to take care of the finest details? That's how God created you—with all the flourishes and features carefully tended to. Not only did he design you specifically to be as fantastic and unique as you are, but God also made you exactly how you are so you can do amazing things for him and for his kingdom.

Make something you love to create today—a picture, a card, a collage, brownies, a video—and as you make it, thank God for making you. As you think through the process, look it over, and add finishing touches. Thank God for putting so much attention into creating you.

And who knows but that you have come to your royal position for such a time as this?

–Esther 4:14

You may not know why you're in the class you're in, why you have *that* assigned seat, why you live in your neighborhood, or why you ride your bus. But God does.

Queen Esther was an orphan. Her entire family had been forced to leave the land they came from. And yet she was chosen as queen. Queen sounds pretty snazzy to us, but Esther didn't necessarily want to be queen. It was frightening living in the same castle as a guy who was as angry, selfish, and cruel as the king. But God put orphaned, exiled Esther in that palace at that time for a very specific reason. God's people, the Jews, were about to be killed, but when Esther got the courage to speak up and told the king what was going on, her entire nation was saved. Wow!

It may sometimes seem random where we've ended up. Sometimes it even seems like bad luck or a punishment. But God has put you exactly where you are for a fantastic reason. He might ask you to speak up or lend a hand or be brave, but God picked you specifically to make a difference right where you are.

~~~~~~~~~~

Is there a place you have to go, a line you have to stand in, a person you have to sit by that has you asking, "Why?" Direct your question to God. "Why, God, am I here? How can you use me? What do you have planned for me in this place?" Then trust him to do something spectacular.

15

The LORD watches over you—the LORD is your shade at your right hand; the sun will not harm you by day, nor the moon by night. The LORD will keep you from all harm—he will watch over your life. The LORD will watch over your coming and going both now and forevermore.

—Psalm 121:5-8

Have you ever been so frightened that you just can't shake the feeling of fear? You might know you shouldn't be afraid of the creak you heard in the middle of the night or of flying in an airplane. Your brain knows it. But it seems to have forgotten to tell the rest of you.

Wouldn't it be great to have a bodyguard standing over your bed at night or sitting next to you in a plane? Wouldn't it bring you peace if you had your own personal escort walking you to and from school, through the neighbors' yards, and the rest of the way home? You do. God is your own personal bodyguard watching over you, protecting you. He's there beside you during the hours the sun is shining. He's there beside you during the hours the moon hangs in the sky. He's there beside you, everywhere you come and go. When fear creeps in, remember you are protected by the most incredibly powerful watchman—God.

~~~~~~~~~~

Write out the verse above on a notecard or piece of paper and tuck it under your pillow. Pull it out on nights you're feeling scared and on mornings of days when you're facing something that frightens you. Read it and be reminded that God is protecting you today and always.

*The Lord is good, a refuge in times of trouble.
He cares for those who trust in him.*

–*Nahum 1:7*

Do you have a hiding place? A place you go when you don't want to be found? It might be in the branches of a tree or on your porch. It might be behind the couch or curled up in your bed. Maybe it's not even an actual "place" but it's when you put on your headphones or go outside and shoot hoops— you can tune out the rest of the world. It's that place that feels safe and separate from everything else. Maybe you go there when you're embarrassed or angry or when you don't want anyone to see your tears. It's a place where you can catch your breath, organize your thoughts, or have a good long cry.

There are times we can't get to our hiding places. Sometimes our secret spaces can't give us all the comfort we need. But God is the perfect refuge. When no one else understands, he does. When no one else is listening, he wants to hear. When you're concerned others will judge you or blame you, God loves you. Whenever you feel like you need your space, that you need time alone, go to God. He's waiting there just for you.

Where do you go when you need to be alone? Why not put a reminder there, that God is your perfect safe place—draw a cross and tape it to the wall or carve one into the bark of your favorite tree. When you feel overwhelmed today, picture that space and picture God there, waiting to comfort you.

Do not store up for yourselves treasures on earth, where moths and vermin destroy, and where thieves break in and steal. But store up for yourselves treasures in heaven . . . For where your treasure is, there your heart will be also.

–Matthew 6:19-21

Milkshakes. The coolest pair of boots. The book or song that's releasing next week. The best smelling lotion. There are so many fun things on this earth to enjoy. And God wants us to enjoy them. You might get allowance or money slipped in a birthday card from your aunt. Maybe you get paid for doing chores. No matter where you get your treasures, it's super important to remember that money—and all the things it buys—are gifts from God.

God doesn't want your money or your things to become more important than him. You can outgrow clothes, get tired of watching a movie, use up a tube of lip gloss, and lose a bracelet. But the most important things last forever. God and his love never run out. You never outgrow hope, faith, and love. Focus on them. It's great to enjoy the things in this world. It makes God smile when you smile. But just make sure you focus on what the most important things in life are.

〜〜〜〜〜〜〜

If you were moving and could only take one thing with you what would it be? Remember that God and his love for you are even more important than that item! Thank God for all of the treasures he has given you and for the fact that his love is the greatest treasure of all.

18

Do not share in the sins of others. Keep yourself pure.

—1 Timothy 5:22

You can learn so much from your friends. They might teach you how to do a back handspring or how to solve tough fraction problems. Your friends might teach you about a new band. But not everything your friends do are things you should do. You are a child of the one true king, Jesus. You are his precious possession. And you should act like it. You weren't created to say bad words. You weren't made to watch inappropriate movies or read trashy books or listen to songs with nasty lyrics. God didn't make you to make fun of others, to make them feel small, to hurt their feelings. And you know this. Because you are chosen by God, and that is a noble thing.

It's not always easy to remember this in the moment—when everyone else is sneaking candy or lying to the teacher about what happened. But these are the exact times that you can be a leader, that you can make a difference. By saying, "No thanks," to bad choices and by saying something kind in the midst of insults, you can teach your friends something—how to live a pure and lovely life.

Was there a time recently when your friends made a bad choice? Did you go along with them or stand up for what's right? Ask God to give you a plan for how to stay true to him the next time something like this comes up. Ask him to give you the strength to follow the plan.

19

Yours, LORD, is the greatness and the power and the glory and the majesty and the splendor, for everything in heaven and earth is yours. Yours, LORD, is the kingdom; you are exalted as head over all.

–1 Chronicles 29:11

When you win the game, get the A, earn the ribbon, have your paper pinned to the bulletin board, or get the solo, what's the first thing you do? Cheer! Give someone a high five!

When things are going great do you take time to thank God? Probably. When things seem same-old-same-old or less than wonderful, do you take time to look around at all of the blessings you have? Maybe not.

Our God is so good and so true and so faithful. He is so incredibly amazing, and he blesses his children (that's you) time and time again! Your day is jam-packed with goodness if you take time to look for it. And all of those fantastic sights, smells, tastes, feelings, and happenings come from God, who loves you very much. When we remember that God is behind all of these incredible experiences, we remember how amazing he is, that God truly is the greatest of all.

Write a list or draw a picture of all the things you're grateful for today. See how many you can think of. It could be a hug or a beautiful sunrise. Maybe it's a crisp apple from the farmer's market or a yummy smelling candle or a giggle with your best friend. Title your list or drawing, "Thank you, God."

20

The grace of the Lord Jesus Christ be with your spirit.

—Philemon 1:25

Grace is the free and undeserved approval of God. God loves you because he made you. In fact, when he looks at you, God doesn't even think about your mistakes, because they were all forgiven when Jesus died on the cross.

Yes, God wants you to be kind and loving, because he is kind and loving, because he knows you're actually happier and more at peace when you are. But God doesn't love you more if you do or say a certain thing. He doesn't love you less if you mess up or forget. You might have to earn your allowance or your GPA or your chair in orchestra, but you don't have to earn God's love. He just gives it to us. He hands it to us like an unexpected present when it isn't even our birthday. And the card reads, "Just for you. Not because of something you've done, but because I love you."

~~~~~~~~~~~~~~~~~~~~

Write God a thank you note for the gift of grace. Thank him for giving you his approval, but also for not asking anything in return. Sign and date your note and slide it in this book. The next time you don't feel like you measure up, read it again, reminding yourself that you already have God's grace.

For Ezra had devoted himself to the study and observance of the Law of the LORD, and to teaching its decrees and laws in Israel.

—Ezra 7:10

Do you have any questions about God? Most of us do! The good news is God has given us a giant book with hundreds and hundreds of pages that teach us all about him. The Bible is packed with answers to your questions. It explains who God is, what he does, and what he can and will do. It explains how much he loves you and why he cares. The Bible is brimming with stories about how God has helped his people in the past, and how he will help you today.

Ezra lived from 480–440 BC. That is a long time ago! But even back then, he was studying what existed of the Bible (the first five chapters of the Old Testament) and encouraging everyone he knew to do the same. Ezra knew there was so much to learn about God in the Bible. We have it a lot easier today than Ezra did when there weren't very many copies of the Bible, and not many people could read. Now the Bible is on sale at many bookstores and websites, and you can even access the Bible for free online or via an app. So start reading today!

Challenge yourself to read the Bible every day this week—maybe first thing in the morning or right before you go to bed. Set up a consistent time, so it becomes routine. Not sure where to start? The Psalms are beautiful. Matthew, Mark, Luke, and John tell the story of Jesus' life and his teachings. Enjoy!

Act justly and to love mercy and to walk humbly with your God.

–Micah 6:8

Today is a fresh opportunity to live for God and to walk fully in his presence. There will be many choices today, so many ways you can please God. When you do what you know in your heart is right, you are walking with God. This might be holding the door for the person behind you or helping someone carry their overflowing armload of books. When you are kind and merciful to others, you are walking with God. This might mean biting your tongue when someone is frustrating, or accepting an apology and letting it go when someone say they're sorry. Maybe it's laughing at a joke even when it wasn't that clever.

When you humbly give God all the credit, because he's the one who gave you your strength, your smarts, your speed, and your skills, then you are walking with God. Maybe someone tells you, "You're so fast!" You can answer, "Thanks. I'm glad God gave me these legs." If you washed the dishes without being asked, don't brag about it, just be happy knowing you did a good thing. You get to choose today. Can you imagine anyone better to walk with than God?

When faced with a decision today, ask yourself: Am I acting justly? Am I being merciful? Am I being humble? If the answer to all of those questions is, 'yes' then you know you're making a good choice. If the answer is, 'no', consider a different way to handle things. Still not sure? Ask God for help.

I can do all this through him who gives me strength.

–Philippians 4:13

There are days when you might feel like giving up, when the mountain in front of you seems too steep to climb. But Jesus promises we can do all things through him. This doesn't mean we can hurt or steal or lie through him. But all the things God created us to do? We can do those things because of him, because he will give us the strength to do them.

If you have a phone whose battery has died and you don't plug it in, it's worthless. It can't do what it was made to do. But if you plug it in, the phone gets instant energy and life. The phone can do the things it was created to do. That's what Jesus is for us—a renewable power source. As long as we stay plugged into him, we can find the strength to try again, the energy to give it another whirl, the courage to stand up to the things in our way. When we plug into Jesus—read the Bible, talk to him, and trust in him—we can do the things we were created to do. All of them.

What in your life seems impossible today? Sketch a picture of a mountain and name that mountain the goal you're trying to reach. Then draw yourself with boots, a rope, and a harness. Label each of these items something you can do this week to start climbing your mountain. Ask God to give you strength.

She is clothed with strength and dignity; she can laugh at the days to come.

—*Proverbs 31:25*

Embrace your personal style. Whether you love cozying up in sweats, dressing up in the latest styles, or rocking cool workout gear, what you wear is a way to celebrate who God created you to be. But no matter how you choose to get dressed each morning, you need to remember who you're dressing for and what that means.

Remember whose attention matters most—God's. Would God like that outfit? Is he okay with you wearing that phrase printed across your shirt or with *that* skirt? Is God pleased you're copying your friends' outfits even though you're more comfortable in something else? Would he want you to leave the house without taking care of yourself? Without brushing your hair or teeth? God sees you and how you present yourself. He made you. He loves you. And God longs for you to dress and care for yourself accordingly. When you remember you are the daughter of the King and that he gave you your own style, it gives a whole new perspective on getting ready each day. It empowers you with strength, dignity, and the ability not to worry about anything this day will bring.

Lay out your outfit for tomorrow. Look it over and ask God, "What do you think?" As soon as the words are out of your mouth, you'll probably know the answer. Now write out today's verse on a sticky note and post it on your mirror, so as you're getting ready, you'll be reminded to wear strength and dignity.

Now this is what the LORD Almighty says: "Give careful thought to your ways."

–Haggai 1:5

God gave you a brain, two feet, and a desire to go. But where you go is up to you. Because God has also given you free choice. The choice to study for your test or to watch your favorite show. The choice to sit with your usual group, or to ask the new kid to join your table at lunch. The choice to say you're sorry to your mom even if you think she started it, or to not speak to her until *she* apologizes. The choice to sleep in on Sunday or to go to church.

Sometimes you know exactly the right decision to make. But sometimes it's hard to decide. It's hard to choose if you should bite your tongue or speak up. It's hard to decide if you should take a risk and welcome someone new into your safe group of friends. But in all decisions, God is there to help you. He asks you to think over your choices—to ask his advice. So whatever decisions you need to make today, ask God for his opinion, think through what he's telling you, and steer yourself accordingly.

List some decisions you expect to make this week with space under each one. They could be big or small. Under each decision write your options. Pray over your choices. As you get answers circle them. Then make those circled choices.

I have not departed from the commands of his lips; I have treasured the words of his mouth more than my daily bread.

—Job 23:12

What time of day are you most hungry? When you wake up? At lunch? When you get home from school, practice, or the sitter's? Do you plan out what you'll eat? Do you ask your parents to get special items from the grocery or to cook certain meals?

Job says he treasures God's word even more than the food he eats. How about you? Do you look forward to reading your Bible—which is the word of God—as much as you look forward to snack or dessert? Do you crave the Bible? What does that even mean? It means that you know when you read your Bible it makes you feel good, it gives you something you need, just like food, and you want more of it. The more you read the Bible, the more it fills that empty part inside. You feel God's love, have more confidence, and have hope in God's plans. The more you read the Bible the easier life seems, because it's a constant reminder that God is right next to you, ready to help in all situations. That he'll never ever give up on you.

What's your favorite food? Would you give it up to read your Bible? You shouldn't skip meals, but reading the Bible everyday should be as important as eating. Today, try reading your Bible before you eat. If that's not convenient, find another time that works, but do make time for God's words. They'll satisfy you more than food.

No temptation has overtaken you except what is common to mankind. And God is faithful; he will not let you be tempted beyond what you can bear. But when you are tempted, he will also provide a way out so that you can endure it.
–1 Corinthians 10:13

Temptations are real and they hit us every single day. Today you might be tempted to yell at your sister, because she always takes sooo long in the bathroom. You might be tempted to *not* take out the trash, because you know your dad will do it if you let it overflow enough. You might be tempted to say a word or watch a show you know you shouldn't when there's no one around to tell you that you can't. Maybe your temptations today will be totally different. But you will be tempted. The good news is God is faithful.

When each of those temptations comes up, no matter how good it looks, no matter how hard it is to say no, God will provide a way out for you, a way for you to avoid making the wrong choice. The Bible also says God won't let you be tempted more than you can bear. That means, everything you're tempted by, God has already given you the ability to turn away from it. You can handle it. You can. All you have to do is ask for God's help.

Is there anything that tempts you regularly? Something or someone you encounter all the time? Ask God for the right words, the right ideas, another path, or another way. Ask God to make it clear what you're supposed to do in the moment of temptation. Then thank him for being so faithful.

28

Love your neighbor as yourself.

–Mark 12:31

Friends. They're awesome. They're challenging. They're fun. They're great, until they're the worst. Because your friends are human, just like you, they'll mess up sometimes (that means sometimes you mess up too). And when you put two people together who both make mistakes, some days there'll be misunderstandings or arguments. Sometimes you'll get on each other's nerves or feelings will get hurt. Don't get me wrong. There will be tons of laughter, stories, and great memories too. Just not all the time.

So how can you be a good friend? By treating others the way you want to be treated. When one of your friends is driving you crazy, treat her the way you would want to be treated if you were driving *her* crazy. Would you want her to scream at you? Talk behind your back? Ignore you? Probably not. Would you want her to talk to you? Find a way to work through the problem? Forgive you for not being aware? Probably. If you like people to wait for you, listen to you, stand up for you, then do the same for your friends and for everyone you meet. Having good friends starts with being a good friend.

Is there someone you struggle with? Maybe because you're super different or competing for the same things or because they seem unkind to you? Think of three things you can do to treat them as you'd like to be treated. Tell them they did a good job or share something with them. Find ways to do those three things this week.

> But the LORD said to Samuel, "Do not consider his appearance or his height, for I have rejected him. The LORD does not look at the things people look at. People look at the outward appearance, but the LORD looks at the heart."
>
> *–1 Samuel 16:7*

Lots of people will tell you who you are. They'll tell you you're not fast enough, not strong enough, not smart enough, too loud, too quiet, too tall, or too short. They'll put labels on you and judge you based on how you look or what kind of car your parents drive. But people aren't qualified to make those judgments. Only God who made you has the right to tell you who or what you are. He knows best, because he's who invented you in the first place. God sees things people never will.

Samuel was looking for a king. He found a man named Eliab that he thought "looked" like a king. But God told Samuel how people look on the outside isn't what matters, it's what's inside. If you love Jesus and long to serve him, your heart is beautiful to him. He loves you and chooses you time and time again to be his prized daughter.

Look in the mirror and pick out your favorite feature. Thank God for your hair, laugh, nose, whatever it is. Now look again and realize that God's favorite feature is your heart. Thank God for it, too, because he thinks it's sensational. Thank God for always thinking you're beautiful, just the way you are.

Remember this: Whoever turns a sinner from the error of their way will save them from death.

—James 5:20

How should you act when you know someone you love is doing something wrong? When your friend posts something inappropriate on social media? When your brother lies to your parents about where he's going?

If you love them, you should help them. Not by covering up what they're doing, but by helping them choose better. This doesn't mean tattling. It means confronting them and suggesting they change. It can be tricky, because you don't want to hurt their feelings, blame them, or make them mad at you. But God will give you courage and strength to challenge their choices.

You won't always get people who are making mistakes to change their minds, but you can always try. And by intervening, you'll know you did the right thing—that you stood up for someone you care about.

~~~~~~~~~~~~~~

Is there someone you care about who consistently makes a poor choice? Pray for them today, that they can feel how much God loves them, that they can have the strength to choose wisely. Ask God to give you the strength and love to encourage this person to make the right choice next time.

Each of you should give what you have decided in your heart to give, not reluctantly or under compulsion, for God loves a cheerful giver.

–*2 Corinthians 9:7*

Open up your hand. Everything you have is a gift God has put into your hand. He gives you time and friends and money and treats and talents and family and sleep. It's hard not to close up your hand sometimes, because what you have is so nice, you want to keep it. But God gives you all of these things so you can enjoy life, help yourself, *and* help others. That means you have to give some of your time by pausing to tie your little brother's shoe or give up some of your money to help the poor or your church. You might have to share a scoring opportunity by passing the ball to a teammate instead of taking the shot yourself.

God wants you to give freely and cheerfully. When you share what God's given you, it always feels good. But if you hold on too tightly, not only will you not be able to appreciate them, but he can't put any new things into your hand for you to enjoy. So keep your hand open. God will continue to refill it with wonderful things.

What do you hold on to too tightly—money, time, the remote? Try letting go a little today. Put aside some allowance for this week's offering. Take a moment to help your mom put away groceries. Let someone else pick their favorite show. When you do, literally open your hands and thank God for all he gives you.

I have told you these things, so that in me you may have peace. In this world you will have trouble. But take heart! I have overcome the world.

–John 16:33

Do you feel overwhelmed? Stressed out? Like you could you use a hug? We all do sometimes. You might lose a game, your homework, or your lunch money. You might run out of time with a long list of things you still need to do. People you care about might let you down or leave.

Some days you just ache inside. Jesus knows all about it. He experienced all kinds of trouble—from being mocked in his hometown to having his good friend betray him while he was here on earth. Jesus gets it. He does. And because he made you and loves you, because he understands exactly what you're going through, he longs to comfort you. Jesus offers you the most loving, strong, soothing hugs. And not only do his hugs feel amazing and make you want to take a long deep breath, but they actually have power.

You can have peace in him, because all the hard, painful, yucky things of the world—Jesus has overcome them all. Step into his arms. Lean into his chest. Let him hug you. Breathe in his peace.

~~~~~~~~~~

Draw a peace sign. In each of the four openings write something you're worried or stressed about. Turn each thing over to Jesus. Ask him to take control of whatever's going on, trusting him to overcome it. Then draw a cross over each of the four things and breathe in the peace Jesus is offering you.

*For all of you who were baptized into Christ
have clothed yourselves with Christ.*

—Galatians 3:27

Each morning you get to decide what to put on. Depending on what the weather is like and where you're going, this will change from day to day. Today might be a jeans and T-shirt day. Or maybe you need to wear your uniform or get dressed up because it's a special occasion. But something you should put on every morning is Jesus.

How do you wear Jesus? Well, think about your clothes—they protect you, they're the closest things next to you, and they're what everybody else sees when they look at you. So, when you start your day with Jesus, ask him to protect you today from hurt feelings and worries and fears. Tell Jesus you want him to be the closest thing next to you today, closer than your friends or your problems.

And no matter where you go or who you see today, try to do and say what Jesus would so everyone around you sees his love when they look at you. Get the idea? Jesus is better than any outfit you own, because when you clothe yourself in Christ, you have everything you need.

As you're getting dressed today talk to Jesus. Let him know everything on your mind. Ask him to protect, cover, stay close to, and shine through you throughout your day. Then whatever comes your way keep reminding yourself you are clothed in Christ.

Suppose one of you has a hundred sheep and loses one of them. Doesn't he leave the ninety-nine in the open country and go after the lost sheep until he finds it? And when he finds it, he joyfully puts it on his shoulders and goes home.

—Luke 15:4-6

Have you ever lost something important and scrambled around like crazy to find it? Some days you might feel like you're losing everything! Do you become crazy when you look for that item? Digging through drawers, asking everyone in your home if they've seen your lost item?

And then how do you feel when you find it? Relieved? Joyful? Do you do a happy dance? Of course you only act that way if the missing item is really important.

Think how hard you search for something important when it's missing. That's how hard Jesus seeks you. He wants to hang out with you and hold you and cheer for you every single day. Any time you ignore him or wander off from him, Jesus starts his search for you all over again, and he won't stop until he finds you. Because you're important to him. Yup, you are so important to Jesus that he'll drop everything to find you. And when he finds you, he'll do a happy dance.

Sit in a quiet place, close your eyes, and ask God to find you. Ask him to sit with you and talk with you. Tell him you're sorry for all of the times you've wandered off, and thank him for always coming to look for you.

35

Finally, brothers and sisters, whatever is true, whatever is noble, whatever is right, whatever is pure, whatever is lovely, whatever is admirable—if anything is excellent or praiseworthy—think about such things.

—Philippians 4:8

Can we talk for a minute about what you've been watching, about what you've been listening to, about what you've been posting? Is it right? Is it pure? Is it lovely? Is it true?

The more you expose yourself to bad words, suggestive pictures, or people making bad choices, the more those things will seem normal to you. Maybe it seems like everyone you know has seen "that movie" or listens to "that band," but that doesn't make it okay. If a TV show makes you uncomfortable, don't watch it. If a song has bad lyrics, stop listening.

God only wants the best for you. He'll help you achieve all kinds of fantastic things, but God needs you to do your part. You need to fill your ears and eyes and heart and mind with excellent, admirable, praiseworthy things. When you do, you'll be able to experience God's love more fully, because there will be less of that other noise drowning him out.

Today, find a way to cut one bad influence out of your life. Maybe it means deleting a song or stopping watching a certain TV show. Maybe it means you need to tell a friend who has been pressuring you to do bad things that you need space. Ask God for the courage to pursue what is right.

Be strong and courageous. Do not be afraid or terrified because of them, for the LORD your God goes with you; he will never leave you nor forsake you.

–Deuteronomy 31:6

Do you remember in the movie, *Dumbo*, when he got a lucky feather? When he held onto that lucky feather with his trunk, he could fly. An elephant could fly?! How? Holding that feather made Dumbo feel brave. It gave him strength to do something that seemed impossible.

Just like Dumbo, you can get through anything too. Not because you have a lucky feather, but because you have something way better—God.

Think you can't make it through this year in science? You can. Because with God you are strong. Think you can't possibly move to a new neighborhood or a new school? You can. Because with God, you're courageous. God is more powerful than anything or anyone and he will never ever leave you. With God at your side you can tackle anything and everything that comes your way.

You are strong. You are courageous. That's how God made you. Spread your wings and fly.

What are you afraid of today? Imagine that thing or person is just a feather in your hands. Now imagine yourself bravely carrying that feather to God and laying it down at God's feet. Ask God to take this fear from you and to remind you to be strong and courageous so you can overcome anything that frightens you.

Shout for joy to the LORD, all the earth, burst into jubilant song with music.

—Psalm 98:4

God wants you to have fun! He loves you so much God wants you to dance and sing and skip!

What makes you laugh out loud? Who makes you smile? If you had an extra thirty minutes every day, what would you do with it? God made you different than anyone else in the entire world and he created things that he knew would delight you personally. Are you doing those things today? If not, what's stopping you?

God wants you to do more of the things that make you happy. He wants you to spend time with people you love. God put all of these wonderful things on your path so you could enjoy them. You don't need a license to have fun, to enjoy life—you just need to get out there and do it. Live your life fully today!

~~~~~~~~~~~~~~~~

Put on your favorite dance tunes and have a dance party with your family or friends. Dance until you run out of breath. While you're at it make sure to thank God for music and fun.

The apostles said to the Lord, "Increase our faith!" He replied, "If you have faith as small as a mustard seed, you can say to this mulberry tree, 'Be uprooted and planted in the sea,' and it will obey you.

—Luke 17:5-6

Is it hard to believe in things you can't see? It doesn't have to be. You can't see love, but you probably know someone who loves you. You know how their love feels—how it can change you. You believe love is real and that it has power.

You can't see the wind, but you can feel its presence, can see how it scatters leaves, bends trees, and waves flags. You believe wind is real and that it has power.

You may not be able to see God, but you don't need to see him to know what he feels like, to see how he can make a difference in your life. Still, some days—the toughest days—it may be difficult to have faith. Luckily, God doesn't ask you to have much faith—just the teeniest, tiniest bit, smaller than a kernel of popcorn. And if you have just a tiny speck of faith, then with God you can do anything.

Go outside. Notice the temperature and the weather. Soak in the warmth or the chill, feel the sunlight, or wind, or drops of rain on your skin. Marvel at how you cannot see warm, cold, wind or wet, yet all of them are real. Thank God for weather and for his very real presence in your life.

"In my distress I called to the LORD, and he answered me. From deep in the realm of the dead I called for help, and you listened to my cry."

—Jonah 2:2

Dot-dot-dot. Dash-dash-dash. Dot-dot-dot.

Long ago it was dangerous for ships to be out at sea because they couldn't communicate with anyone. If they were lost they couldn't call anyone for directions. If they were sinking, they couldn't call anyone to ask for help. When the telegraph was invented, ships put machines on board so they could call for help if they were in danger.

The above combination of dots and dashes translates into the letters "S.O.S." in Morse code, the alphabet of the telegraph. In 1908, S.O.S. was chosen as the international distress signal, similar to our 9–1–1. Many people today think S.O.S. stands for Save Our Ship, and it kind of does, but it actually developed because it was so easy to type and recognize on telegraphs.

When you're in trouble you don't need a cell phone or a telegraph. You have God. He hears you no matter how you spell or what language you speak. And he'll answer you.

Dots in Morse code are quick taps. Dashes are long taps. Think of a prayer request you have, something you want to talk to God about. Now talk to God about it. Then, try tapping out an S.O.S. to him. Dot-dot-dot. Dash-dash-dash. Dot-dot-dot. With each tap, know God is always listening to your prayers.

Then hear from heaven, your dwelling place.
Forgive and act; deal with everyone according to
all they do, since you know their hearts (for you
alone know every human heart).

—1 Kings 8:39

Did you see her haircut? Why did he say that? Can you believe how she acted? Because other people were uniquely created by God, sometimes they won't be anything like you. Kids in the cafeteria might eat things you hope never show up in your lunch. The rules at friends' homes might be different than your family's rules. Sometimes the various ways others dress, talk, or act is just because they do things differently than you do.

But no matter why other people are different, it's not your job to criticize them. You'll never know their whole story, but God does. The teacher who's always late to school might live far away and is doing her best to get there on time. The boy who wears the same thing every day might not be able to afford more outfits. And since God knows every single person's heart, including yours, he's the only guy qualified to judge. Your job is to be the best *you* you can be.

———

List three people who are very different than you, who you have a hard time not criticizing. Pray for each one of them. Pray that they can feel God's love, that they can know God better. If you know something specific they're struggling with (like grades or problems at home), you can pray for that too.

The LORD bless you and keep you; the LORD make his face shine on you and be gracious to you; the LORD turn his face toward you and give you peace.

–Numbers 6:24-26

Parents might yell at you. Instructors and coaches might criticize you. Teachers might shake their heads at you. The bus driver might grumble at you. Neighbors might stare at you. Your friends might laugh at you. Even your cat might run into the next room and hide under the bed when you want to pet her.

But God? He will always stand right beside you, loving you, shining on you, truly understanding you and why you do everything you do. When you mess up, God will steer you back to what's right. When you forget, God will help you remember. When you fall, God will help you get back up. When you fail, God will give you the strength to try again. So, no matter what else anyone else has to say, even when you have no idea how people are going to react, there's no question how God will act. God will be gracious to you.

Change the word "you" in the verse above to "me" and pray it out loud. "The Lord bless ME and keep ME; the Lord make his face shine on ME and be gracious to ME; the Lord turn his face toward ME and give ME peace. Amen."

Moreover, when God gives someone wealth and possessions, and the ability to enjoy them, to accept their lot and be happy in their toil—this is a gift of God.

–Ecclesiastes 5:19

Everything you can buy wouldn't exist if it weren't for God. God gave inventors the ideas to create new technology. God brought rain and sunshine down to the earth for crops to grow. God gave authors inspiration to write books. It's hard to remember when you're eating your favorite tacos that God created all the ingredients and even your taste buds, making it possible for you to enjoy your favorite foods. But he did!

So you can choose. Each time you get something new, you can look at it as something you earned or deserve. You can give people all the credit, or you can also thank God. It just takes a little thought. You might be thinking, "Wow, this sweatshirt is so cool! I love this brand—they have the best styles. It's so cozy. I'm lucky to have a grandma who buys me surprises." All you need to do is add a few thoughts like, "I'm so grateful God gave someone the idea to make this sweatshirt, that he gave me a sweet grandma, and that he made it possible for me to have this sweatshirt."

Don't forget to thank your grandma too!

Look around your room. Everything in it is a gift from God. Your aunt bought your bedspread and you won that trophy at your swim meet. God gave your aunt the resources to buy your comforter and he helped you win your race heat. Thank God out loud for each item.

This is the message we have heard from him and declare to you: God is light; in him there is no darkness at all.

–1 John 1:5

Recess would be great if you didn't have to pick up all of the balls at the end and put them away. Corn on the cob is delicious, if only it wouldn't get stuck between your teeth. Dinner is awesome, except when you have to eat your veggies (especially if they're Brussels sprouts). You love gymnastics, but having to do pull-ups during warm-ups is the worst.

So many of the things we love have bad parts—parts we have to deal with to enjoy the good stuff. But with God, there aren't any bad parts. He's loving and kind and good and wise. He's always there for you and never lets you down. He's always strong enough, smart enough, and bright enough. He has all of these awesome qualities in the good times and in the bad times. With God there aren't any crusts to cut off, any parts to skip, or anything to "get through" to get to the part you like best.

God is the best part! And because God is always good, you can always trust in him and his ways.

~~~~~~~~~~~~

Close your eyes and imagine the feeling when you study hard for a test and get an A, or when you practice your free throws over and over, and in the game, you make the shot. Let that feeling wash over you. That is goodness. God is pure goodness. Let God's goodness wash over you.

Seek good, not evil, that you may live. Then the
LORD God Almighty will be with you, just as
you say he is.

—Amos 5:14

When you play hide-and-seek, you don't just stand there and wait for your friends to come out of their hiding places. No, you look all over to find your friends. You'll look under beds, in closets, maybe even in the clothes hamper. You probably do it eagerly, trying to find them all as quickly as you can.

God asks us to seek good. That means not just answering the question when the teacher calls on you, or putting your clothes away when your dad asks you to. Those are nice things. They are *doing* good, which God calls you to do. But that's like waiting for your friends to come out from behind the curtains. There's a difference between doing and seeking. And God asks you to do more than just do good; he also asks you to seek it. Are you looking for ways to help, to make a difference, to be a friend, to make someone smile? Seek goodness and God in all of his goodness will come alongside you. He'll even help you find some more.

Write down two ways you can intentionally seek goodness today and tomorrow. Ask God for ideas. Could you draw a picture for someone? Write them a note? Maybe you could do someone else's household or classroom chores? Enjoy how good it makes you feel when you seek good.

45

And I pray that you, being rooted and established in love, may have power, together with all the Lord's holy people, to grasp how wide and long and high and deep is the love of Christ, and to know this love that surpasses knowledge—that you may be filled to the measure of all the fullness of God.

—Ephesians 3:17-19

In rainy season, the Amazon River can get up to 25 miles wide! It's the widest river in the world, but God's love is wider. The Great Wall of China is 13,170 miles long. It's so big, it can actually be seen from outer space! But God's love is longer. The Grand Canyon is more than 6,000 feet deep, but God's love is deeper.

We use measuring sticks, scales, and tape measures to measure things on earth, but God's love is so enormous, there isn't a tool big enough to measure it. That means God's love can't be blown away by bad news, stomped on by a bully, washed away by your mistakes, or overpowered by anything or anyone. God's love is so great and so grand that it towers over everything else. And this amazing love? God offers it to you, each and every day.

What's the tallest building or mountain you've ever seen? Could you reach the top? What's the deepest pool or lake in which you've ever swam? Were you able to touch the bottom? Thank God for his great love, and that you'll never be able to reach the top or bottom of it.

The LORD your God is with you, the Mighty Warrior who saves. He will take great delight in you; in his love he will no longer rebuke you, but will rejoice over you with singing.

–Zephaniah 3:17

Is there someone you love to be around because they make you feel special? Maybe it's your grandma, because she always listens to everything you say, and she makes your favorite dessert whenever you come over. Maybe it's the teller at the bank, because whenever you're there running errands with your mom, this particular person says hello, remembers your name, and gives you candy in your favorite flavor.

For as much as these people seem to delight in you, for as excited as you are to see them, God delights in you infinitely more and is excited to see you. God always wants to talk to you, to sing with you, and to protect you. God will find a million ways to make you smile, because he chooses you and God is always excited to be with you.

How can you make God feel special too? You can pray to him. You can sing to him. You can go out and help others. You can tell your friends about him. Any time you make a difference in someone else's day, you make God smile.

You shall have no other gods before me.
—Exodus 20:3

What's the most important thing to you? Your grades? Your looks? Your new pair of shoes? Your friends? Your sport or activities? Your phone or tablet? How much time do you spend on that thing? How often do you talk about it, or think about it?

Now . . . how much time do you spend with God? The same amount? Maybe not.

When God gave the Ten Commandments to the Israelites, he warned them not to have "idols." You might think of an idol as a golden statue, and you probably don't have any of those. But anything that becomes more important to you than God, that comes before him in your life, is an idol. God loves you, wants to spend time with you, and asks you to put him first.

Make an appointment with God first thing tomorrow morning. If you have a calendar or daily to-do list, schedule God in before you do anything else—before you eat your breakfast, brush your teeth, check your phone, anything! When you make God first, you're off to an amazing start!

48

There is no fear in love. But perfect love drives out fear.

–1 John 4:18

God is louder than thunder. God is stronger than a tornado. God is more powerful than an enormous crashing wave. But you never, ever have to be afraid of God.

Even if you've done something embarrassing, something that makes you feel bad, something you hope no one ever finds out about, God loves you. He's on your side. God doesn't want you to be hurt by your actions. God wants to guide you to do better. God wants to heal you so you can move on. When you tell God about it, when you tell him you're sorry, that you don't know what to do, God will take away all of your fear, and fill you with his beautiful, incredible, enormous love.

God is the mightiest, strongest, most powerful being that exists, but he's on your side. God doesn't want you to be afraid of him, because there is nothing to be afraid about when it comes to God. He loves you. Perfectly.

Close your eyes super tight. That thing you can't believe you did or thought or said? Talk to God about it, like he's your very best friend, because he is. Tell him you're sorry. Ask him how you can move forward. Let God wrap his love around you.

49

In your unfailing love you will lead the people you have redeemed. In your strength you will guide them to your holy dwelling.

–Exodus 15:13

Your mom packed you an apple, but you'd rather eat the cupcake. Your partner on your science project didn't do any of the work. Should you tell your teacher or do your partner's share of the assignment? There will always be decisions to make, some of them harder than others, but you never have to make them alone.

When it matters, God will lead your heart and mind to choose wisely. When it's important God will always help you discover the best decision and how to do it. All you have to do is:

1. Ask for God's help
2. Read the Bible. See what God's Word has to say about your situation.
3. Choose the way he shows you.

God's answers might not come at the snap of your fingers, but they will always come in time, and they will always be best.

Start a prayer journal. Write down today's date and any decisions you might be facing. Follow the steps above. If God gives you any signs, jot them down too. If you don't get an answer today, that's okay. Write it down again tomorrow, and again seek God's guidance. .

*If you declare with your mouth, "Jesus is Lord,"
and believe in your heart that God raised him
from the dead, you will be saved.*

–Romans 10:9

Do you have to read the Bible every day? Nope. It's a great idea, and you'll get to know God even more every time you do read the Bible, but God doesn't give homework assignments.

Do you have to go to church *every* Sunday? God loves it when you go to church, because you can learn so much about him there, and hang out with other people who also want to know more about God and act more like him. But God doesn't take attendance. (If your parents tell you to, you should honor them.)

Are there any certain verses you need to memorize? No. God gets excited when you have Bible verses in your head, because then you can remind yourself how much he loves you when things are challenging, but God doesn't give tests.

Then what do you have to do to get God to love you? To go to heaven? To have your sins forgiven? It's so easy. All you have to do is accept Jesus as your Lord and believe that he really did die for your sins. That's it. God's love is that easy to get and it's always waiting for you.

Have you asked Jesus to be your Savior? Do you want him to be the most important thing in your life? If not, ask him now. If so, tell him again. It's as easy as saying, "Jesus, I love you. I want you to be my king. I believe you're God's Son, and that you died for my sins. Amen."

But Ruth replied, "Don't urge me to leave you or to turn back from you. Where you go I will go, and where you stay I will stay. Your people will be my people and your God my God."

–Ruth 1:16

Has your mom ever yelled at you? Has your brother ever blamed you for something you didn't do? Do you ever get frustrated having to share everything with your family— the bathroom, the backseat, the brownies? Living in close quarters with different personalities can sometimes be challenging.

But God gave you a specific, unique family so you have people to rely on, laugh with, lean on, learn from, and experience life with. You, and your family—you're in on this together. If your arms are full, your family can help you carry your load. If you feel like the world is crashing down, your family can embrace you in a warm, loving hug. If something hilarious happens, your family will listen to your story and laugh with you over and over again.

Because God gave you the special family you have, he asks that you support them, help them, forgive them when they're sorry, and freely give them your love. The cool thing is, they'll do all of those same wonderful things for you.

~~~~~~~~~~

Draw a picture of your family or write down all of their names. Think of a way you could make each person in your family smile today. Now, go do those things.

To him who is able to keep you from stumbling and to present you before his glorious presence without fault and with great joy—to the only God our Savior be glory, majesty, power and authority, through Jesus Christ our Lord, before all ages, now and forevermore! Amen.

—Jude 1:24-25

You may have heard fairy tales about queens and their bejeweled crowns, but Queen Elizabeth II is a real live queen. Queen Elizabeth II is Queen of the United Kingdom and fifteen other countries. She is the longest reigning British king or queen ever. Her crown contains more than 3,000 jewels.

But even someone as famous as Queen Elizabeth II has nothing on God. Queen Elizabeth II is human. God is perfect. God doesn't just have power over a list of countries; he reigns over the entire universe. God's rule isn't measured in years, because it lasts forever—he can never lose his throne. And God's crown? Well, he created shooting stars, waterfalls, and rainbows; it's hard to imagine how sparkling and colorful his crown must be.

The best part? God is *your* king. He is your ruler. God will watch over you and keep you safe, and he does it with great joy, because he loves you.

Draw the kind of crown you think God wears. Be creative. When you're finished, read out loud the verse above from the book of Jude praising God for his majesty.

Therefore, there is now no condemnation for those who are in Christ Jesus, because through Christ Jesus the law of the Spirit who gives life has set you free from the law of sin and death.

–Romans 8:1-2

When you make mistakes, there are usually consequences. If you don't turn in your homework, you might get a zero. If you scream at your sister, you might be asked to clear her dishes for a week. If you forget to return your library books, there might be a fine. If you shove a player from the other team, you might have a foul called on you.

But with God, when you make mistakes, there is no punishment. He won't ground you. He won't stop talking to you. He won't withhold something from you. Sure, God will try to teach you better behaviors, try to remind you to be more responsible, to make good choices, but God will never ever harm you. He is never ever mad at you. Jesus took all of the punishment for all of your mistakes, so you don't have to be afraid of what God will think or what he will do to you. Yes, God longs for you to live for him and with him, but when you slip, God is there to pick you up. God loves you and wants what's best for you. Always.

What kind of punishments have you received—being grounded, losing your allowance, failing a test? Tell Jesus thank you for taking all of the penalties you deserve for your sins. If there's anything you're feeling guilty about right now, ask God to forgive you and know in your heart that he already has.

You need to persevere so that when you have done the will of God, you will receive what he has promised.

–Hebrews 10:36

Some things take a lot of work!

You might practice a piece of music for months before perfecting it. You might work for weeks researching, practicing a presentation, and making a poster for a history project before turning it in. Along the way there will be days when the music sounds flat or you need to erase something on your poster. On those days it might feel like the hard work is pointless. You might be tempted to give up.

But when you work for God, there will always be a reward. God has given you specific talents, has given you unique tasks, and has assigned you special work that only you can accomplish. Because God has appointed you to this particular work, he asks you to never give up. Never stop trying, standing up for what's true, doing what you know in your heart is right, or talking to God about everything. God is faithful and keeps his promises to take your efforts and use them for good.

~~~~~~~~~~~~~~~~

Is there anything you're working on right now—a goal you're trying to achieve, or a problem you're struggling to overcome that seems like you'll never accomplish? Write it down. Ask God to show you what's next. Jot down any ideas that pop into your head. Commit to doing one of those things this week.

The grass withers and the flowers fall, but the word of our God endures forever.

—Isaiah 40:8

What's the big deal with the Bible? It was written thousands of years ago and talks about people without TVs, cell phones, or cars. How could it possibly apply to you?

Are you ready? The Bible was written by God for you! That's pretty awesome. God had humans write it down, but he told them what to write. All the things God included in the Bible are things he wants *you* to know. God only chose the events, the stories, and the people that he knew would teach you and encourage you and show you more about who he is and how much he loves you. The people in the Bible loved their families but fought with them. The people in the Bible got hungry, jealous, scared, tired, overwhelmed, and sad. The people in the Bible loved God and wanted to follow him, but messed up over and over again. Can you relate?

The Bible may have been written a long time ago, but God wrote it for you. The truths contained within its pages never expire and never go away. The Bible is as real and meaningful today as it was when it was written.

———

Do you have a Bible? If not, ask your church if they have free ones they give away (many do) or download a free app that gives you a Bible. Pick a verse or two you like and highlight or underline them, knowing that God wrote them just for you!

For you are a people holy to the LORD your God. The LORD your God has chosen you out of all the peoples on the face of the earth to be his people, his treasured possession.

–Deuteronomy 7:6

Other people's words can hurt . . . a lot. At a parent/teacher conference your teacher might tell you she's disappointed in your effort. A coach may reprimand you for stumbling on the beam or on the court. Your friends might say something you do is silly or dumb. You might even put yourself down when you don't do well on a test. But no matter what anyone else says (including yourself) God says you are his treasured possession!

God decided to make you, and he made you exactly how you are. He has chosen you out of all of the people on the earth to be his special daughter. That means that all those things other people might say, how they might treat you, how they might make you feel—they don't mean a thing. Because to the most powerful, amazing Lord of all, you are priceless.

~~~~~~~~~~

Go look in the mirror. Tell yourself ten times in a row, "I am God's treasured possession. God has chosen me." Emphasize a different word each time. So, the first time say: I am God's treasured possession. The second time say: I AM God's treasured possession, etc. Let the words sink in one at a time.

Do not forget the covenant I have made with you, and do not worship other gods.

–2 Kings 17:38

Have you ever gotten someone's autograph? Met someone famous? Is there a singer, athlete, or actress you follow on social media or wish you could be like?

It's fantastic to have role models. People who use their God-given talents for his glory should interest us and excite us. They should motivate us to do the absolute best with the gifts God has given us. But we shouldn't idolize these people. Famous people get zits, have bad hair days, and get runny noses. Just like us, they fall down, scrape their knees, get mosquito bites, and sometimes make bad choices.

If there's an Olympic runner who wows you with her dedication to training, that's super. Look to her for ideas on how to structure your workouts. If there's a singer whose songs always make you happy, awesome. Listen to her lots and smile. But remember those celebrities were created by God, just like you. They are not better people or more important than you. They're just different. And when you're looking for advice on how to act or who to be, know that Jesus is the ultimate role model.

~~~~~~~~~~~~~~~

Is there anyone famous you adore? How much time do you spend listening to their music, watching them play, or scrolling through their accounts? Every time you want to check out your favorite celebrity this week, why not check in with God first? Read God's Word, talk to him, and breathe in his gorgeous creation.

And everyone who calls on the name of the LORD will be saved; for on Mount Zion and in Jerusalem there will be deliverance, as the LORD has said, even among the survivors whom the LORD calls.

—Joel 2:32

You didn't mean to, but you said something hateful to your sister, something you know hurt her. In the moment you were so angry it just blurted out. Now you've made her cry and you feel horrible. You didn't mean to, but you were practicing your cartwheels in the family room and you kicked over the lamp. It cracked, but you put it back and your parents haven't noticed . . . yet. You feel so badly—you know it was expensive. You know they'll be upset.

There is probably something you've done that you regret, that you wish you could redo, undo, or just make disappear forever.

There's good news. If you ask Jesus to forgive you, he will. All you have to do is call out to him. It's that easy. You'll need to apologize to your sister about what you said and to your parents for the lamp. There might even be a consequence. But between you and God, everything is set right.

Write down something you're ashamed of on a scrap of paper. Ask God to forgive you for what you did and to help you not do it again. Now rip up that piece of paper into tiny bits. Throw them away or flush them down the toilet, knowing that as far as God's concerned that thing is gone forever.

I care very little if I am judged by you or by any human court; indeed, I do not even judge myself.
—1 Corinthians 4:3

When you go to a friend's house, do you start comparing? Sizing up how big her closet is compared to yours? Considering the color of her walls, the smell in her kitchen, the size of her TV, how clean her house is, or what's in her backyard compared to yours? Sometimes it makes you wish you had more of what she has. Sometimes it makes you feel like you're better than her, because of how your home is different.

But God asks us not to compare ourselves to anyone else. God made you exactly how you are and he made your friend exactly how she is. He gave her the home, possessions, and family she has. God gave you your specific living situation and all of the things you have for a purpose. You never have to worry about proving yourself to your friends, or how your room compares to theirs. Have a clear conscience that God knows you so well, that he made you exactly how you're supposed to be, and he put you exactly where you were meant to be, so that he could do amazing things through you.

Take a look around your home today with fresh eyes. Write God a thank you note for all of the special things about the space you live in—all the things that make it feel like home to you. Make sure to tell God thanks for knowing you so well that he gave you just what you need.

60

Keep your mouth free of perversity; keep corrupt talk far from your lips.

—Proverbs 4:24

What is "corrupt talk?" Pretty much anything you wouldn't want your teacher or parents to hear you say. Words you definitely wouldn't want your grandparents or youth pastor hear you say. They might be curse words—the ones that make a movie R-rated, ones that get you sent to the principal's office. But there are other words that have ugly ideas attached to them—words that make fun of people for how they look or where they're from.

The point is, you know what these words are. Sadly, you probably hear them all of the time. Your best friend might even use them, might even be allowed to say them in her house. But just because you hear them, doesn't mean you ever have to speak them. You are a child of God. You are chosen by him. He loves you and takes pride in you. Don't you want your words to glorify him?

Are there any words you know you shouldn't say, but say anyway? Think up alternative words or phrases for them. They could be plain, like "dang," or so silly they'll get you and your friends giggling, like, "oh, monkey toes!" Start using these better substitute words when you're tempted to use bad ones.

61

"You are the salt of the earth. But if the salt loses its saltiness, how can it be made salty again? It is no longer good for anything, except to be thrown out and trampled underfoot."

–Matthew 5:13

What's your favorite salty food? Can you taste it? Imagine a potato chip or French fry or whatever you're imagining without the salt. It's still a chip or a fry, but *ew!* It tastes bland, flat, like it's missing something important. And when you bite into it, it isn't quite what you'd hoped for. That's how a person is without Jesus in their life. They're still them, they're just missing something—the something that makes them fully special, brings out their best.

Jesus says, "You are the salt of the earth." Yes, you! That means you get to help others find their full potential. You can show them by sprinkling a little kindness their way and by giving them a dash of forgiveness. You can show others how to be complete by being open about your faith. And when your saltiness rubs off on others, then they can learn how to become the best versions of themselves too.

Do you know anyone who could use a little salt? Who isn't quite living to their full potential? Ask God to help you show that person a dash of God's love this week.

Now faith is confidence in what we hope for and assurance about what we do not see.

—Hebrews 11:1

Have you ever wished you had a crystal ball to see your future, or that you could shake a Magic 8 ball and ask, "Will we win?" or "Does Jacob like me?" or "Will I make it through my speech without trembling?"

Neither imaginary crystal balls nor toy Magic 8 balls can truly answer questions about your future. But God knows all the answers, exactly how things will turn out. In the end, he's victorious.

No matter what you're unsure of, you can be certain God is there for you and always will be. Knowing God is on your side means you don't have to worry if you'll win your game. You don't have to worry about who likes you; you can be certain God loves you. If you get nervous during your presentation, you can have faith God will get you through that speech and through anything else you face.

So even when you can't see what's next, God can. Walk with him and trust him to guide you through all the unknowns you have to steer through each day. You may not have all the details, but God does. And in the end, Christ triumphs and your eternity is with him.

~~~~~~~~~~

Is there anything in your future, you can't see, but would like to know about? You can ask God about it right now. Ask him what steps to take, how to serve him in this situation. Ask God to help you in the best ways. Have faith he will guide you through, all the way to the end of time.

Now when Daniel learned that the decree had been published, he went home to his upstairs room where the windows opened toward Jerusalem. Three times a day he got down on his knees and prayed, giving thanks to his God, just as he had done before.

–Daniel 6:10

Do you pray before mealtime at home, but not in the cafeteria or when you're out to eat? Do you pray before bed every night, except when you spend the night at a friend's or away at camp? Are you afraid what someone will say or think if they see you praying? Or are you just not sure how to go about it in a different place than you're used to?

Daniel knew he could be thrown into a den full of hungry, angry lions for praying, but he did it anyway. Daniel wasn't worried about what anyone thought when he prayed, because he knew God was his best friend, that God's opinion was the one that mattered most. Daniel knew that talking to God helped him with everything he faced. Daniel knew praying gave him peace, comfort, courage, and joy. Why would he give that up? Praying can bring you peace, comfort, courage, and joy too. There shouldn't be anything, not even a little discomfort, that should make you want to give up taking time to talk to God, the one who knows you best and loves you most.

Is there anywhere you are uncomfortable praying? Why? Talk to God about it and ask him for courage to overcome your uncertainty. Then next time you're out of your comfort zone, pray anyway. Who knows, maybe one of your friends will join in.

If we confess our sins, he is faithful and just and will forgive us our sins and purify us from all unrighteousness.

–1 John 1:9

Have you ever stained your clothes? Spilled green paint in art? Dribbled chocolate sauce off your spoon? Splattered mud? That stain is dark and obvious and a reminder of your mistake. But you show it to your mom and she puts stain stick on it, soaks it, scrubs it with extra detergent, and when it comes out of the wash, your shirt looks new. You look for the stain and can't find it. You rub your fingers over the area where you know the stain was, but there isn't even a trace of it. It's amazing!

Even more amazing is the fact that this is exactly what Jesus does with your sins. He treats them, soaks them, and scrubs them clean, so that no one can see them anymore, not even God. He totally and completely forgives you. Jesus died on the cross for your sins, and when he did, he got rid of all of your stains once and for all, leaving you clean and bright—just like new.

~~~~~~~~~~~~~~~~

Is there a mistake you've made that you can't let go of? Imagine that sin as a stain. Then imagine Jesus putting you in the laundry. When you come out, you are shining and bright, and even though you search for the mark where the sin left a stain, there isn't even a trace of the spot. You are forgiven.

> *There is a time for everything, and a season for every activity under the heavens . . . a time to weep and a time to laugh, a time to mourn and a time to dance.*
>
> *—Ecclesiastes 3:1,4*

In the movie *Inside Out*, Riley's family moves forcing her to leave her home, friends, and team. Her emotions go bonkers! In the end, Riley realizes all her feelings need to work together to be whole and fully happy. *Inside Out* is just a movie, but it gives us a peek at the emotions God gave us and how he wants us to use them. God created happy, sad, excited, angry, hopeful, and disappointed, and he wants us to express them all while touching base with him to make sure we use them wisely.

On sad days, it's okay to cry. When you're offended, it's okay to feel angry and respectfully express how you feel. On funny days laugh out loud. When you miss someone, look at pictures of them or write them a letter. And on days you achieve or get chosen, celebrate. All these feelings work together to make us who we are, to help us fully experience life. Jesus felt all of these emotions too. He wants you to express the feelings he gave you. It's part of how God made us human. So, cry when necessary, because soon you'll be ready to laugh and dance!

What emotions are you feeling today? Write a journal entry to God telling him how you're feeling and what's causing you to feel that way. Know that God loves you and that he cries and laughs right alongside you.

We are not trying to please people but God.
–1 Thessalonians 2:4

Have you ever been in the middle of telling a story, and then a guy you know sits at the table, and you stop telling it? Or you're making funny faces with your friends when a boy walks by and what was hilarious a second ago is all of a sudden embarrassing? Or you're out and about with your family and your mom says, "Isn't that _____ (fill in the blank with a boy's name you know)? Why don't you say hi to him?" And you think, *Mom, that would be awkward!*

Boys are different than girls. They act and react differently. Not because they're weird or wrong, but just because God creates each of us uniquely, and part of that includes making guys different than girls. But just because they're not the same, doesn't mean you have to change how you act around them or worry about what they think. You are still you, the awesome girl God made you to be. Whether you're with a group of girls or a group of guys, be yourself, at all times. No matter who you're with, or who's around. Let your awesome self shine brightly.

~~~~~~~~~~

Think of a time you've acted differently around a boy. Imagine yourself in the same scenario not changing who you are at all—saying hi if you typically say hi, staying just as loud or quiet as normal, working with them as a partner. Ask God to help you stay true to the person he made you to be.

> Jesus looked at him and loved him. "One thing you lack," he said. "Go, sell everything you have and give to the poor, and you will have treasure in heaven. Then come, follow me."
>
> –Mark 10:21

In the verse above, Jesus tells a specific rich man, who loved money way too much, to "sell everything." Jesus doesn't ask *you* to sell everything *you* have, but he does ask you not to get too attached to cash.

Jesus knows money is a necessary part of life on earth—we have to work for it, it's how we pay bills, and how we buy things. But Jesus also knows if you value money too much, it becomes a problem. When you become greedy, you can lose sight of the important things like your faith, your family, or your friends.

Just like everything you have, money is a gift from God. God doesn't want you to clutch or cling to cash, but to use it wisely for your needs and to be aware of the needs of others. Mostly, God wants you to put him first, above everything, even money.

~~~~~~~~

How could you share some of your money today, so you don't hold on to it too tightly? Maybe put some money in the church offering, or in your classroom fund. Maybe you could buy a small gift—gum, a bookmark, a marker—for someone special. Thank God for money and ask him how he wants you to use it.

How can you say to your brother, "Brother, let me take the speck out of your eye," when you yourself fail to see the plank in your own eye? You hypocrite, first take the plank out of your eye, and then you will see clearly to remove the speck from your brother's eye.

–Luke 6:42

In a band everyone has an instrument. Each instrument needs to be tuned, or it will sound flat or off pitch. Each musician is responsible for tuning their own instrument, because they don't understand each other's instruments well enough to do it properly.

The same goes for your life. Everybody needs to work on something, but you can't understand fully what's going on with others or the best ways for them to improve the melody of their lives. Luckily, you don't have to worry about anyone else's behavior. But God does want you to trust him as he helps you fine-tune your actions. God asks you to work to your full potential instead of nit-picking others.

With God's help you can play the most beautiful music, and as he works with the people around you to tune their lives, together you can live in harmony.

~~~~~~~~~~

Ask God right now how you can fine-tune your life. Ask him to help you stop worrying about what other people need to fix about themselves, and instead have him help you focus on how you can be the best version of yourself.

For you were once darkness, but now you are light in the Lord. Live as children of light.

—Ephesians 5:8

Have you ever tried to find your way in the dark? Maybe stumbling through the garage until you find the switch on the wall or shuffling from your bed to the bathroom in the middle of the night. There's an uncertainty about darkness. Places that are familiar in the light seem farther, sharper, or steeper. Noises in the dark sound louder, more sinister. You probably don't think twice about walking around in the light, but in the dark you second-guess your steps so you don't bump or fall. That dog barking is harmless in the light, but in the dark, the same noise might give you a start.

Living life without Jesus is like bumbling around in the dark. Jesus is The Light. He is like a flashlight on a camping trip, headlights on a dark road, and sunbeams bursting through a stormy sky. He brightens everything, makes life easier to see and understand. Without Jesus, we're not sure where we're going or what to do next, but with him we can see clearly where we are, where we're headed, and how to get there. Jesus is warm and glorious. Let him shine on you.

~~~~~~~~~~~~~~~

Close your eyes and try walking across the room (be careful). Now open your eyes, go back to your starting point, and walk across the room in the light. Take a moment to write down or think about the differences. Thank Jesus for being your light. Ask him to shed light on your life today.

Who shows no partiality to princes and does not favor the rich over the poor, for they are all the work of his hands?

—Job 34:19

Does it seem like the kids whose dads know the basketball coach always get the most playing time? Like the kids who live in a certain neighborhood have cooler backpacks? Like the girls who hang out in *that* group are everyone's favorites?

In your day-to-day life some people might get preferential treatment over others. But God doesn't work like that. God doesn't judge you by what you wear or where you live. God doesn't rate you by your grades or how you wear your hair or what activities you are or aren't involved in. God made you with his own hands. He made you exactly how you are and he loves you exactly how you are. He picks you for his lineup and to play in his orchestra. If God had a screensaver, your face would make it in the picture. It's hard to imagine that God adores all his children. But it's true. That includes you. God adores you!

Make a list of your favorite things—your favorite color, flavor of ice cream, maybe your favorite song or book. Think of how fantastic all of the things on your list make you feel. Know that God feels the same way when he thinks about you. Thank God for loving you that much.

*Because your love is better than life, my lips will
   glorify you.
I will praise you as long as I live, and in your
   name I will lift up my hands.
I will be fully satisfied as with the richest of
   foods; with singing lips my mouth will
   praise you.*

—Psalm 63:3-5

If only you could sit next to your best friend in class, then schooldays would be way cooler. Except then it wouldn't be so fun to catch up together at lunch.

If only your dad didn't work so late, you'd get to spend more time with him. But actually, if Dad worked the early shift, you might not see him in the mornings.

If only you could get an A on this paper, you'd be satisfied with your grades. But actually, there will always be more homework, more tests, and more papers.

Worldly accomplishments or changing our circumstances will never be enough. The next best thing might temporarily make us feel better, though they will never be a permanent fix. But Jesus? He's not only enough—he's better than life. When you hang out with Jesus, you won't have that longing for just a little something more, because you'll already have everything you've ever needed.

If you could change one thing about your current life what would it be? Ask Jesus to help you stop worrying about it and start understanding how to handle this thing. Thank him for being the answer to all your prayers.

Praise him with timbrel and dancing, Praise him with the strings and pipe.

—Psalm 150:4

It's so fun to plan celebrations! Treats need to be baked and tasty dips and snacks need to be prepared. Decorations—like streamers, balloons, and twinkling lights—need to be set out and arranged. Sometimes playlists need to be compiled, games organized, speakers set up, and candles lit. There is excitement in the air.

All of the planning and preparing for a holiday or event can be a blast. God asks us to praise him with the same energy and enthusiasm. He asks us to dance and play instruments and go all out! So whether it's an Easter brunch, Christmas Eve, a youth event at church, or your mom's birthday, go all out, get into the spirit of the occasion. But make sure you are directing your praise and passion not only to the special event, but also to God who made it all possible.

What's your favorite part of planning a celebration? Do you like to bake, wrap gifts, or make cards? Do one of these things today, but do it for God. Maybe that's cleaning under your bed and telling God you want things to look nice for him, or gathering flowers in a vase while thanking God for nature.

73

Likewise, the tongue is a small part of the body, but it makes great boasts. Consider what a great forest is set on fire by a small spark.

—James 3:5

Have you ever spilled a cup with barely any water in it that went everywhere? Just when you think you've wiped it all up, you find more has dripped onto your chair and the floor. How could such a small amount of water make such a mess?

Just like liquids seem to spread farther than seems possible, unkind words spill out and spread much further than we intend them to. When we say we think someone is too loud, had a lousy throw, or joke they must be stupid if they didn't know the answer, those words drip into hearts and souls. Someone you criticize might doubt themselves on the next quiz, in the next game, or stop raising their hand. Or the unkind words might make them angry—causing them to lash out and speak unkindly to someone else.

When we spill, we can only clean it up after the accident. But we don't have to wait until unkind words have spilled out of our mouths to wipe them up. We can proactively choose kind words so there's no mess to clean.

Intentionally choose kind words today. Prepare by thinking of positive phrases to use in the situations you know you're most likely to "spill." If you're tempted to say something mean, bite your tongue. Pause. Ask God to help you either stay silent or interject with something kind.

So Shadrach, Meshach and Abednego came out of the fire . . . They saw that the fire had not harmed their bodies, nor was a hair of their heads singed; their robes were not scorched, and there was no smell of fire on them.

—Daniel 3:26-27

Shadrach, Meshach, and Abednego decided to choose differently. The king made a golden statue and commanded *everyone* to bow down to it. Choosing God over the king meant being in danger. The punishment for not bowing down was being thrown in a fiery furnace.

But Shadrach, Meshach, and Abednego said no. They decided not to serve anyone except God. The king threw them in the furnace, but God saved them. They weren't hurt at all.

If you aren't on social media, you might miss posts. If you don't watch a show, you won't understand the conversation about last night's episode. You might miss out.

But that's okay. Because when you walk with Jesus, he'll make sure you know everything you need. He will pull you out of your tough spots. He will save you. He won't leave your side, and you'll come out unharmed.

Is there anything you are feeling pressured to do? Ask God right now to give you the strength to say no—to stand up to the pressures and temptations in life. Thank him for never leaving your side.

I will pour out my Spirit on all people.

—Joel 2:28

Are there days when it seems nobody cares? When your parents are busy with work, or your best friend is home sick from school so you're not sure who to sit next to in social studies? Days when the teacher never seems to notice that your hand is raised, or when everyone's artwork is on display except for yours?

Even when no one else seems to be paying attention, God is always paying attention to you. God is never too busy. He never misses what you're doing. God pours his Spirit out on *all* of his people—the ones who get called on and the ones who don't, the ones who tell long, hilarious stories and the ones who prefer to sit and listen. God's love for you is available when you're making good choices and when you mess up. God is for you on your best days, to celebrate with you, and on your worst days, because those are the days he can help most.

No matter how you feel about yourself, God thinks you're amazing. He loves you and wants to do great things through and with you. His Spirit is for all people and that includes you.

~~~~~~~~~~~~~~~~

Make a list of the first ten people you think of. Leave a space after each. They can be people you do or don't know, people you do or don't get along with. In the space after each one, write your name. Over each name (including all ten of yours) write, "God's love is for you."

Now you are the body of Christ, and each one of you is a part of it.

–1 Corinthians 12:27

Bees make honey, pollenate flowers, and are responsible for pollenating one out of every three bites of food you eat! The work of a bee is incredibly important, but a single bee can't do anything by itself. Bees need each other. A bee colony consists of 20,000–80,000 bees! Queen bees lay eggs, creating more bees. Drones mate with the queens, enabling them to fertilize the eggs. Most bees are worker bees—all with different jobs. Some clean the hive, some take care of the baby bees, some build the honeycomb, and others guard the hive, to protect the honey.

Just like bees in a hive, each human has a job within the body of Christ—that includes you! Some are good listeners, full of ideas, great at explaining things, or making people feel good. Some of God's children are musical, great with numbers, or talented at making things work. But God has gifted everybody with a special role in spreading God's love. Just like bees, you aren't called to do it alone. Use your gifts today to make a difference, and together Christians can sweeten the world.

~~~~~~~~~~

Spend a few minutes researching bees today. As you think about each of their jobs, consider how God has gifted you— what he's calling you to do for his kingdom. Thank God for your special talents and ask him how he'd like you to use them today.

You should not gloat over your brother in the day of his misfortune.

–Obadiah 1:12

There's one in every crowd. The bully. The snob. The interrupter. The know-it-all. And when they mess up or get caught or punished you might laugh or think, *finally.* But God created those people just like God created you.

You don't know what another person's life is like. You don't know what pressures have been put on them or what they've been through. And because you can't know where they're coming from, it's not fair for you to put them down or cheer when that person fails.

You've probably been unkind once or twice. You might have bragged about something before. Most likely there's been a situation when you felt like you knew better than those around you. We all mess up. But fortunately, Jesus isn't a punisher. He's a savior. And just as Jesus forgives you for all of your mistakes, he forgives everyone else for theirs.

Is there anyone who is really hard for you to like? Pray right now that God will help you see that person through his eyes, that you will better be able to see them as a child of God. While you're talking to God thank him for forgiving you for your mistakes.

Reaching into his bag and taking out a stone, he [David] slung it and struck the Philistine on the forehead. The stone sank into his forehead, and he fell facedown on the ground.

–1 Samuel 17:49

Everyone faces giants. Your giant might be an instructor, coach, or peer who intimidates you. Your giant might not be a person—it might be a disability, an illness, a problem—something that makes life difficult. You might encounter roadblocks that seem to stop you from getting where you want to go and how you want to get there. The thing you're up against is huge! But no matter what giant you're facing—God is bigger.

God equips you and prepares you with everything you need. Sometimes you'll think, *This isn't enough—I'm not strong enough, tall enough, smart enough, trained enough, brave enough.* But all David had when fighting the giant were five smooth stones. And they were more than enough to win the battle because David had God on his side. You also can't take on obstacles by yourself, but with God and all of his power, might, and wisdom, you can strike down your giants. You can overcome them. Because God's on *your* side. And he is bigger.

Take inventory of the "stones" God has given you. Are you fast? Funny? A problem solver? Creative? How can you use these gifts to overcome whatever seems to be blocking your way? Ask God for guidance in making a plan to conquer your giant this week.

"Go and enjoy choice food and sweet drinks, and send some to those who have nothing prepared. This day is holy to our LORD. Do not grieve, for the joy of the LORD is your strength."

–Nehemiah 8:10

How does an ice-cold lemonade make you feel on a hot summer day? What does a sweet, spicy apple cider make you think of? How can a rich, creamy hot chocolate change your mood?

When you're having a crummy day, God asks you not to grieve but to find strength in his joy. What does that mean? That means, it's okay to be sad or angry, but it's not okay to stay in that grumbly spot. It means God has promised you so much—that he will always love you, always be there for you, always cheer for you, always listen to you, always understand. It means that God is bigger than all of your problems and has created so many things for you to delight in—such as cocoa. So when things look dreary, you can talk to God about them, and then allow his light to shine in. His love can change you from sad to happy, discouraged to excited, but you have to ask him for ways to find strength and joy. Savor all the sweet things God has put in your life and let his love put you in the very best mood.

Make yourself a lemonade or cocoa today. While you're at it, make a second or third one to share with someone you care about. Sip the sweetness together while talking about and thanking God for all of the sweet things he gives you both to enjoy.

The LORD God took the man and put him in the Garden of Eden to work it and take care of it.

—Genesis 2:15

What are your favorite things in nature? Butterflies? Streams? The smell of freshly mowed grass? Do you like to collect interesting rocks or seashells? Identify trees by their leaves? God made the entire earth and everything in it. And God asks us to take care of it.

You can care for the earth by reusing things—like wearing your jeans an extra day (if they didn't get dirty) or refilling an empty bottled water the next time you need a to-go drink. These reduce the amount of water, laundry detergent, and plastic going into the environment and save money too.

You can use reusable containers to pack your lunch or carry groceries, so you aren't using as many plastic or paper bags. This reduces the trash that ends up in our world. You can also turn off the water while you brush your teeth, reducing the use of a natural resource.

Almost every worksheet, empty yogurt container, and cereal box can be recycled. Make an effort to throw them in the recycle bin, doing your part to protect the earth. Reusing, reducing, and recycling are great ways to show God how much you care about his creation.

~~~~~~~~~~

Draw a picture of your favorite thing in nature. Thank God for creating that thing for you to enjoy. Intentionally reuse, reduce, or recycle something today to protect the things you love, and all of God's creation.

But the fruit of the Spirit is love, joy, peace, forbearance, kindness, goodness, faithfulness, gentleness and self-control.

—Galatians 5:22-23

If you have accepted Jesus as your savior, then all the fruit of the Spirit are alive and growing within you—love, joy, peace, forbearance (that's a big word for patience), kindness, goodness, faithfulness, gentleness, and self-control. They're all there. Right now. And you have the ability to feel these things, to be these things 100 percent of the time.

They're like shoes in your closet. They can help you, but you have to intentionally put them on your feet. Ballet slippers help you dance. Slippers warm your toes. But they can't do their job if you leave them in your closet.

The same is true with the fruit of the Spirit. They're yours. You own them. They were a gift from God. If you're struggling to be kind to you-know-who, you can dig into your heart and intentionally slide on kindness. If you're feeling impatient while waiting in line or for dinner, ask God to help you tap into the patience that's already yours, and you'll find the waiting much easier. The fruit are in your heart, just waiting to be worn.

What fruit of the Spirit do you struggle tapping into the most? Write down: I have _____. I am full of _____ (fill in both blanks with the fruit you struggle with most). Ask God to help you reach for this fruit whenever it seems difficult.

82

The ways of the LORD are right; the righteous walk in them, but the rebellious stumble in them.

–Hosea 14:9

As Little Red Riding Hood set out to Grandmother's her mom warned, "Stay on the path!" In *The Hobbit*, Gandalf the wizard's last words to Bilbo and his dwarf friends as they reached the edge of the forest were, "Stay on the path."

Little Red started on the path, but was tempted away by beautiful wild flowers. Straying from the path gave the evil wolf the perfect opportunity to sneak over to Grandmother's. Not good. The hobbit and his crew also began on their path, but strayed off when tempted by campfires and the smell of yummy food. As soon as the travelers stepped off the path they became lost and in danger.

God loves a sense of adventure, but God also warns you to explore from the safety of the paths he has paved for you. When you stay on God's roads you'll walk and run and get where you're headed. When you stray, and let bright lights and pretty things distract you from God, you'll stumble. Stay on God's path today, and you'll experience more than you ever imagined possible.

~~~~~~~~~~

Has anything tempted you recently to do something that's not part of God's plan for you—not on God's path for you? Tell God about it now. Of course, God already knows about it, but he's waiting for you to talk to him. Explain why it tempted you. Ask for strength to clearly see his path and stay on it.

Suddenly an angel of the Lord appeared and a light shone in the cell. He struck Peter on the side and woke him up. "Quick, get up!" he said, and the chains fell off Peter's wrists.

—Acts 12:7

Chances are you probably don't wake up on early days without some nudging. Does your mom come in and shake you? Do you have an alarm clock or set the alarm on your phone? Does your dog lick your face? When you know someone or something is set to wake you, you can sleep peacefully without worrying about getting up on time.

The same is true with waking up for God each morning. You want to follow God's call. Live for him. And just like your trusty alarm clock, God will shake you and wake you and show you which choice he wants you to make, which decision is in line with his will. Some nights you might double check your alarm or ask your mom one more time if she'll wake you. But you never have to wonder if you'll hear God when he calls. God's battery will never wear out. He won't ever forget. God didn't let Peter sleep through his plans to rescue him from jail. God had an angel shove and speak loudly to Peter to make sure he was awake. Know God won't let you miss any of his plans for *you*, either.

~~~~~~~~~~~

Write down a decision you're trying to make or something you're wondering about for your future. Ask God to make clear his will for you. Jot down any ideas that come to mind while talking to God. Thank God in advance that he'll wake you up to his plans loud and clear when the time is right.

No weapon forged against you will prevail.
—Isaiah 54:17

Gabby Douglas was the first African-American woman to win the Olympic gold medal for the individual all-around in women's gymnastics. But there were so many obstacles in her way, many wondered if she would prevail. Gabby's parents were separated. Her mom was sick. Her family was poor. Gabby had to leave her home in Virginia for two years and live with a host family in Iowa to receive the training she needed. There she got incredibly homesick. She suffered injuries. Life was never easy.

And yet, she triumphed. What did Gabby have? What got her through? Faith in Jesus. Gabby grew up going to church, reading the Bible, and praying when times were tough. And times were tough but God was tougher. No matter what seems to be opposing you today, God is stronger. God promises NO weapon forged against you will prevail. Not anyone's opinion or any circumstance you face will defeat you. In fact, when Jesus places a desire in your heart you'll be able to flip and jump high over the hurdles that come your way. Your challenges will shrink in the shadow of God's greatness.

List any obstacles you feel are in your way—anyone or anything that seems to be stopping you from living out your full potential. Ask God to clear them out of your way, then cross each one off your list, confident that God is stronger, and with him you will triumph for him and for his glory.

Teach us to number our days, that we may gain a heart of wisdom.

—*Psalm 90:12*

Do you ever count down the days until Christmas or your birthday or vacation? Does it sometimes seem to take forever, like the days are passing by in slow motion, to get to the awaited day?

Every day God wants to teach you something, share something with you, and have you experience something wonderful. During the Christmas season, the days of decorating the tree, baking cookies, or crafting cards is all part of the fun. You wouldn't want to skip those things would you? God is excited for our celebrations, but with God every single day counts. God will use every practice to prepare you for games and every rehearsal to help you learn your lines for opening night. In the same way God will use every single day to allow you to discover delicious flavors, happy giggles, comforting hugs, and quiet moments in which he can remind you how very much he loves you.

No matter what you're looking forward to today, make sure you're not overlooking where you are right now.

What are you looking forward to? Ask God to show you ways to enjoy today, tomorrow, and each day leading up to that big day. Write at least two things you can do between now and then on your calendar or planner.

86

*But you are a chosen people, a royal priesthood,
a holy nation, God's special possession, that you
may declare the praises of him who called you
out of darkness into his wonderful light.*

–1 Peter 2:9

In a presidential election, the country gets to vote for who they want as president—for who they think the best person is to guide the country. At school, you might get to vote for student council members. You're supposed to vote for who you think will best represent your class. A team might get to vote for team captain, someone the team members think will lead the team with great attitude and work ethic. The people elected, those who win the vote, are chosen.

So are you. But you are chosen by someone far more important than your classmates or teammates or even more than the population of the United States. You are chosen by God. God votes for you. God picks you. Every single day, he fills out his ballot and says, "*You*, you're the one I want to love. You're the one I think is special. You're the one I want to help. You're the one I want to spend time with today."

You are chosen by God. Let that sink in today.

Go look in the mirror and say out loud, "I am chosen by God. I am royal and holy in God's eyes. I am God's special possession." Write at least one of those phrases on a sticky note and put it on your mirror to remind you all over again how awesome God thinks you are.

Each one should test their own actions. Then they can take pride in themselves alone, without comparing themselves to someone else.

—*Galatians 6:4*

Social media can be a blast—motivational quotes, gorgeous pictures, catching up with your favorite people. But social media can be dangerous. If you start rating yourself or your life based on what others are doing, you'll lose sight of the incredible person God created you to be.

Most people only post highlights—the time they won the award, the day their hair looks fantastic, or the cool place they visited. Few people post about studying spelling words or making their bed, about losing or struggling. What you see on social media is only what others want you to see. Remember, the girls who went to the concert still have chores to do.

But even if they didn't, it wouldn't matter. No matter what others post, no matter how many hearts or likes you do or don't get on your posts, you are loved and cherished by the creator of the universe. God thinks you are amazing! So comparisons are pointless, because you've already been liked, hearted, retweeted, and gotten two thumbs up by the King of Kings.

～～～～～～～

If you're on social media, post something about Jesus today. Post a favorite Bible verse, or a sunrise, or your best friend, thanking Jesus for that wonderful thing or person in your post. If you're not on social media just tell someone, "I'm thankful to Jesus for . . ." That's like a one-on-one post. I promise Jesus will "like" it.

The ravens brought him bread and meat in the morning and bread and meat in the evening, and he drank from the brook.

–1 Kings 17:6

Do you have a pet or a classroom pet? When does it get fed? Does it have a special dish or bottle for water? Does its cage need to be cleaned out? Does it need to go for walks or need to be held? You love your pet and you want it to be taken care of. You want your fish to have a clean tank and your horse to get its exercise and your cat's collar to be secure. You want to play fetch with your dog and snuggle with your bunny.

Even more than you look out for your pet, God looks out for you. Even more than you love your pet, God loves you. God makes sure you have everything you need to love and to serve him. When Elijah was in the desert, God sent ravens carrying food in their beaks to feed him and set him near a stream so Elijah had water. Talk about room service! God will take care of your needs too. He'll never forget what you need to thrive for him, because he created you. He'll do anything it takes to care for you in all the ways that truly matter.

What do you feel like you need today? Hope? Energy? Self-control? Motivation? Tell God about it. Tell him what you think you need and why. Ask God to help you, to give you exactly what you need to live for him. Thank him in advance for providing it.

A gentle answer turns away wrath, but a harsh word stirs up anger.

—*Proverbs 15:1*

What makes you angry? The bully who teases the quiet girl at recess might make you angry. Maybe it's a sibling who always seems to hog the remote or the backseat. Or perhaps the family who always picks you up late for carpool, which makes you late for practice (even though you were ready on time), makes you angry.

It's natural to get frustrated sometimes. It's what you do with that anger that's important. God asks us to speak gently, to steer away from harsh words. That means even when you're upset, you shouldn't shout or slam a door. You shouldn't ignore the person who's making you mad or shove him or her or talk badly about that person to others. You can ask the bully to leave the girl alone. You can kindly ask your sibling to share. You can explain to your coach that whenever that family drives you'll be a few minutes late. God will help you with this. Wherever you're headed, whoever you'll see, choose gentleness today.

~~~~~~~~~~~~~~~~~~

Is there someone who consistently upsets you? Sit down with Jesus and tell him about when and why this person angers you. Then ask Jesus to take all the angry feelings away. Ask him to give you calmness and gentleness toward this person and your situation.

His master replied, "Well done, good and faithful servant! You have been faithful with a few things; I will put you in charge of many things. Come and share your master's happiness!"
—*Matthew 25:23*

God has gifted every single person he created with different talents. He's made some people logical and some people creative. God gave some people the gift of listening and others the gift of talking. He never judges you on what you're good at, because he put all of those abilities in you in the first place. But God does want you to use those strengths, those special gifts, to glorify him.

If you're a gifted writer, God wants you to not only embrace your English homework, but to possibly write positive articles for your school newspaper or youth group website. If you've got a knack for computers, God might ask you to help when the Internet crashes or when your sister needs help downloading something for class. If you're a talented cook, maybe God wants you to prepare some meals for your family or a church event.

There is so much you can do with the talents God gave you. Go out and use them to make a difference today!

List your talents. Struggling? Ask someone who loves you to get you started. Thank God for your abilities, then ask him how you can use them to glorify him. Write the ideas down. As you think of more ways to use your gifts in the days to come, add them to your list.

So then, just as you received Christ Jesus as Lord, continue to live your lives in him, rooted and built up in him, strengthened in the faith as you were taught, and overflowing with thankfulness.

—Colossians 2:6-7

Roots are important to the health and survival of a plant. Roots actually anchor a plant into the dirt, keeping it in place so rain or wind can't sweep it away. Roots also grow down into the dirt, searching for food and water. The water and nutrients the plant gathers from its roots get pumped up to the stems and leaves through photosynthesis to feed and hydrate the plant.

Jesus feeds you truth—that you are loved, that you are chosen, that you are forgiven, that he will give you everything you need. And then he holds you in place. Because if you understand how loved and cherished you are by Jesus, then it's easier to make good decisions, to follow God's plan for you, and to stay grounded in who he created you to be.

Draw a picture of a green, leafy plant above the ground with long roots growing down into soil packed with plant food and water. Label the soil, "Jesus." Label the plant with your name.

> *"Bring the whole tithe into the storehouse, that there may be food in my house. Test me in this,"* says the LORD Almighty, *"and see if I will not throw open the floodgates of heaven and pour out so much blessing that there will not be room enough to store it."*
>
> *–Malachi 3:10*

If you ate an apple down to the core then gave somebody that core, would that be generous? Sure, that core might be 10 percent of the apple, but you'd know it was useless. Nobody wants to eat a core, except maybe a goat.

God gives us everything we have—from apples to allowance. All he asks in return is that we "tithe," or give one-tenth back to him. If you earn $10, God asks you to give him $1 back. Giving back to God can take many forms—the offering basket at church, a canned-food drive at school, a Saturday spent cleaning up a park. You can decide where with the help of your parents and God.

If you're hesitating returning 1/10 to God, consider if someone handed you that apple core. How would you feel? God deserves our best, not our leftovers.

Give him back a "tithe," and God not only promises that you won't miss what you give, but also that he'll bless you.

Create a special place where you will set aside your tithes—it could be an envelope, a basket, or maybe a bowl. Store one-tenth of your money there. Also, write down some ideas for sharing one-tenth of your time and put them in this same place.

And Elisha prayed, "Open his eyes, LORD, so that he may see." Then the LORD opened the servant's eyes, and he looked and saw the hills full of horses and chariots of fire all around Elisha.

–2 Kings 6:17

Helen Keller lost her sight and hearing when she was only 18 months old. Left in the dark, she understandably became angry and emotional. She felt incapable of being able to learn, explore, or express her feelings. When Helen was seven, Anne Sullivan came to teach her. Anne devoted her life to helping Helen communicate—first with sign language and later with Braille. Anne could not give Helen her physical sight back, but it was as if she opened Helen's eyes to understanding the world around her.

Helen went on to graduate from college with honors and create organizations which spread awareness and helped people with disabilities. She won numerous awards for her humanitarian work.

God takes us out of dark places and helps us to *live*—to better understand and appreciate the world around us, to introduce us to new people, new experiences, new ways to experience his love and grace, and more amazing ways to live for him. Open your eyes today to what he wants to show you.

~~~~~~~~~~~~

Set a timer for three minutes. Sit with your eyes closed and your ears covered. When time is up, journal about how it felt without sight and sound, and what a difference it made when you went back to fully using your senses. Ask God to make you more aware of all he has in store for you.

Honor your father and your mother, so that you may live long in the land the LORD your God is giving you.

—Exodus 20:12

Parents listen to you, tell you stories, get you where you need to be, and make you spaghetti with extra sauce. But some days, your parents might seem too busy. Some days they might seem like they don't understand. Some days they might seem to expect too much from you. Others they might seem like they're not paying attention at all.

Parents are human, so they don't always get everything right. But even when they're wrong, you're still called to *honor* them. What does that mean? That means speaking respectfully to them, answering their questions, lending a hand around the house, and following the rules they've set up in your home. Even if you think they're crazy sometimes, remember that your parents love you. They're trying their best. They want you to be happy and healthy, and their rules and suggestions are meant to help you succeed.

Make a list of five things you love about your parents or guardians. Thank God for each of the things on your list.

Do you not know that your bodies are temples of the Holy Spirit, who is in you, whom you have received from God? You are not your own; you were bought at a price. Therefore honor God with your bodies.

–1 Corinthians 6:19-20

How do you see your body? How do you treat it?

Do you eat right? That means making sure you get enough calories to fuel all your activities each day, and the right kind of calories—ones that come from whole grains to give you energy, loads of fruits and veggies to give you the nutrients that make your body work, and proteins to build your muscles.

Do you drink six to eight glasses of water a day to stay hydrated?

Do you exercise? Do you move and groove and stay active to keep your heart pumping, your brain charging, your bones and muscles strengthening, and to keep germs away?

Do you get enough rest, so your body can reset, recharge, and be ready to go tomorrow?

God created your body, and he considers it a temple. Shouldn't you do the same? Treat your body with honor and respect today and every day.

~~~~~~~

Choose one of the healthy tips above and write it down. For example, if you don't drink much water, you could decide to drink a glass with every meal and snack this week. Focus on loving and caring for the wonderful you God created.

So God created mankind in his own image, in the image of God he created them; male and female he created them.

—Genesis 1:27

Have you ever tried to make something out of Play-Doh or clay? You have an idea of what you want it to look like in your mind, but as you bend, shape, and mold the dough, it ends up looking a little lumpy, too flat, or not quite as you intended.

What if you could take that clay and shape it exactly as you imagined, if you could form it into anything you like? God can do that. He can create anything he wants and make it look exactly as he imagines. God could have made you look like anything. He could have given you five ears or feathers or gills or horns. But he intentionally chose to create you in his image, to illustrate his awesomeness. What an incredible honor, that God would love you enough, appreciate you enough, and adore you enough to want you to reflect him.

You were created in the image of God. Let that sink in today.

~~~~~~~~~~

Create something today—a drawing, brownies, a flower arrangement—anything! As you assemble the colors, ingredients, or stems, thank God for assembling each of your features exactly as he did.

97

Do you not know that in a race all the runners run, but only one gets the prize? Run in such a way as to get the prize.

–1 Corinthians 9:24

I'll race you!

How do you feel when you hear those words? Do you change how you run if you're running against a classmate, a teammate, or a sibling? Do you run differently if you're tired, if it doesn't count, if someone's timing you, if there's a prize for the winner?

God wants you to run to him. And not just run, but run as fast as you can, run like you're racing, run like the Olympics depend on it, run as if a gold medal awaits you at the end. Because the best prize imaginable is a life with God. And the harder you run toward him, the sooner and more often you'll experience the peace, love, hope, and joy that come from being with him.

~~~~~~~~~~~~~~~~

Grab a friend, family member, or neighbor and race them today. It could be a running race, a hopping race, a race on scooters, whatever you like. As you race, pay attention to how you think, how you move, how you focus. As you race toward God, race like that.

For I am convinced that neither death nor life, neither angels nor demons, neither the present nor the future, nor any powers, neither height nor depth, nor anything else in all creation, will be able to separate us from the love of God that is in Christ Jesus our Lord.

–Romans 8:38-39

You are not alone. You don't have to go through anything you're challenged with by yourself. If you've lost someone you love, if you had to move away from something you care about, if you made a mistake and the consequences are harsh, if you're sick, or if you're facing something new that fills you with uncertainty, you do not have to go it alone. Jesus is always with you.

Nothing can separate you from God, or him from you. No person, no misunderstanding, no amount of miles, no money owed—nothing can separate you from God. So no matter who you have to face today or what you have to do, you can do it because Jesus is at your side. And he's cheering for you. No matter how hard it gets, he will never stop.

What's the hardest thing you're going through right now? Talk to Jesus about it. Ask him for strength and courage and wisdom. Remember that nothing can separate you from him.

Therefore, since we are surrounded by such a great cloud of witnesses, let us throw off everything that hinders and the sin that so easily entangles. And let us run with perseverance the race marked out for us.

—Hebrews 12:1

How do you feel when your hair gets tangled? When it's in a knot, and you brush and brush, and the knot seems to get tighter, and it hurts like crazy as you try to untangle the mess?

Does your life ever feel tangled? Like when you're in a fight with someone and neither of you will apologize first? Or when something you do turns out to be the wrong decision?

Just like that knotted up hair gets worse and worse the longer we wait to comb it out, our mistakes can get messier the longer we let them go. But as soon as we turn our faults and failures over to Jesus, he begins to untangle our lives. Sometimes we need to be patient, and sometimes it's a little uncomfortable, but when Jesus is finished, the rough spots of our personalities are smoother, our sharp, grumpy edges softer, and our dull parts (the ones that are afraid to stand up or take chances) shine brighter.

Does anything have you tangled up inside? Something you said or did? Turn it over to Jesus right now. Imagine your mistake like a knot of hair, and picture him using a brush to untangle it. Stay with this thought until it's completely untangled and you are free.

100

Then they called them in again and commanded them not to speak or teach at all in the name of Jesus. But Peter and John replied, "Which is right in God's eyes: to listen to you, or to him? You be the judges! As for us, we cannot help speaking about what we have seen and heard."

—Acts 4:18-20

Because she believed that all people deserved equal treatment, Rosa Parks refused to give up her seat on a bus. That seems like no big deal to us, but Rosa was arrested for speaking her mind. Rosa Parks sparked a national movement towards equal rights, and later received a Congressional Gold Medal.

Peter and John were threatened by their government for speaking about Jesus. Because they believed in him, Peter and John told as many people as they could about Jesus, even after they'd been told not to.

Would you stand up for your belief in God if someone else was making fun of church, youth group, or the Bible? If someone asks you why you say "gosh" instead of "God" or why you bow your head before eating your snack would you tell them why?

You will have chances to stand up for what you believe. And if you do so in the right way—with respect, patience, and thoughtfulness—you can make big changes too.

Thank Jesus for who he is, for how he loves you, for how he saves you, for how he'll never leave you. Ask Jesus for strength to stand up for him today and every day.

And now, dear lady, I am not writing you a new command but one we have had from the beginning. I ask that we love one another.

–2 John 5:5

Jesus asks that we love one another.

He doesn't ask us to love some people. He doesn't ask us to love sometimes. He doesn't ask us to love when we feel like it, when someone is nice to us, or when we're in a good mood. He asks us to love one another. Period.

That means when the principal makes a new rule that seems ridiculous; you're supposed to love her. That means when someone cuts in front of you in line, you're supposed to love them. That means when your brother teases you, you're supposed to love him. Jesus doesn't say that it will be easy, but he does ask us to do it. Why? Because we all mess up. We all have that moment where we're unlovable. So just like we hope people will love us even when we're acting grumpy, we're supposed to love others when they're not at their best. And if everyone loved everyone all of the time, well, life would be pretty amazing.

Sure, not everyone else will always love you, but it has to start somewhere. And Jesus asks that it start with you.

━━━━━〜〜〜〜〜〜〜〜━━━━━

Is there someone who you find unlovable? Write down three nice things about them. Ask Jesus to help you see that person through his eyes. Make an effort to see the best in that person this week and show them love and kindness.

I am the Alpha and the Omega," says the Lord God, "who is, and who was, and who is to come, the Almighty."

–Revelation 1:8

In most of the movies you've seen and the books you've read, the beginnings and the ends are the most important parts—they're the parts that show what the story is going to be about and how all of the pieces finally fit together.

When you were little you probably learned "The Alphabet Song." And even when you weren't sure what order all of the letters went in, you probably got A and Z right—the beginning and the end. In the Greek alphabet, Alpha is like our "A" and Omega is like our letter "Z".

God said, "I am the A and the Z—the beginning and the end. I'm why and how it all got started—the world, your life, everything. I'm also how all of the pieces fit together, how the problems get solved, how the wrongs are made right, how everything makes sense." God was with the world before it was created, is with you every second of now, and will be with all of creation to the very end. Find strength and comfort in his security and constant presence today.

Write out you're ABCs, but replace "A" and "Z" with the word God. Now write three sentences about yourself and replace any "a" or "z" with God's name. Notice how important he is to your life and thank him for being the God who's always there.

Every good and perfect gift is from above,
coming down from the Father of the heavenly
lights, who does not change like shifting
shadows.

—James 1:17

Can you breathe today? Did you eat any meals? Are you wearing clothes? Of course those are things you expect each day, that are part of your day, but can you imagine your life without air or food or clothing? Every single gift you experience comes from God—everything.

It's God's gift when the sun is in the sky providing you light to go about your day. When you notice a beautifully colored leaf or the sweet song of a bird. When you get a ride somewhere you wanted to go. When there's still hot water when it's your turn to take a shower. When you're feeling sick and you're able to stay home from school and rest. When you understand the new concept in math. When your pillow feels soft under your head. These are all gifts from God.

And yes, bad things will happen. But God will sprinkle so many good and perfect gifts into your day that they will outweigh the bad and make things better, more comfortable, and happier. Keep your eye out for all of the gifts he gives you today.

~~~~~~~~~~~~~~~~

On Day 19 you made a list of things you were thankful for. Either pull out that list or start a new one. Throughout the day jot down the good and perfect gifts you notice God has given you. Make a habit out of it. Challenge yourself to add to it every day this week.

So we fix our eyes not on what is seen, but on what is unseen, since what is seen is temporary, but what is unseen is eternal.

–2 Corinthians 4:18

The people of Pompeii had a heated pool, crosswalks, and fast food restaurants. Pretty amazing considering they lived almost 2,000 years ago! They thought they had everything, but in the end none of their stuff could save them. In 79 A.D., the entire population of Pompeii died when Mount Vesuvius erupted. There wasn't anything they could do.

Today there are volcanologists who can predict when volcanoes will erupt. People living near a volcano could vacate and be safe prior to an eruption. But modern society still gets hooked on technology and having the latest and greatest of everything. There's absolutely nothing wrong with getting new and improved things—with enjoying what life has to offer, but when things become more important than God, there's a problem.

Even though you may see the coolest stuff at the mall there's nothing cooler than Jesus. Everything else becomes outdated, breaks, or eventually needs to be replaced. Stay focused on Jesus. He'll always be with you and will never need an update.

What are your most valued possessions? Go through your list one by one and tell Jesus you want to love him more. Thank Jesus for always being there for you and for lasting forever.

The angel said to those who were standing before him, "Take off his filthy clothes." Then he said to Joshua, "See, I have taken away your sin, and I will put fine garments on you."

—Zechariah 3:4

Have you ever gotten hot and sweaty or played outside and gotten filthy? How soon did you take a shower and change? If you didn't have time to clean up right away, how did you feel? Sticky? Itchy?

That's the same way it feels if you stay in your sin. If you feel badly about something and ask Jesus for forgiveness, he forgives you. Jesus says, "Why don't you take off those filthy clothes of sin? Let's get you cleaned up." Then he hands you soft, fresh, comfortable clothes to change into.

Feeling guilty about hurting someone's feelings or being sneaky is natural, because it's a reminder that God is good, and he longs for you to be like him. It should motivate you to do better next time. He wants you to learn from your mistakes, not dwell on them.

~~~~~~~~~~

1. Draw or imagine a picture of yourself wearing dirty clothes. Label the clothes with anything you're struggling forgiving yourself for.
2. Draw Jesus handing you clean clothes.
3. Imagine yourself putting on the fresh outfit Christ offers.

Then Moses stretched out his hand over the sea, and all that night the LORD drove the sea back with a strong east wind and turned it into dry land. The waters were divided, and the Israelites went through the sea on dry ground, with a wall of water on their right and on their left.

—Exodus 14:21-22

The Israelites were trapped. Behind them the well-trained Egyptian army charged towards them on 600 chariots. In front of them was the Red Sea, over 169,000 square miles of water. It seemed there was no way out.

Have you ever felt like you were at a dead end?

God whisked the water right out of the way of the Israelites and made a clear, dry path for them. They walked safely through with walls of water on both sides. Their enemy followed in hot pursuit. But once the Israelites were safe, God tumbled those walls of water right on top of the Egyptians.

Whatever you're facing today, God has a safe path planned for you. Trust him. Follow him. Stay right with him and he will move water out of the way, clear that path for you, and keep your enemies from overtaking you. Just trust him one step at a time.

───────

Is there anything that has you feeling trapped today, anything keeping you from following God's path? Close your eyes and picture that thing resting at the edge of the ocean. Now imagine God carrying it away in a giant wave. Thank him for always providing a safe path for you.

107

"I will be a Father to you, and you will be my sons and daughters, says the Lord Almighty."

–2 Corinthians 6:18

In your mind, how would a perfect father act?

Maybe when you had a story to tell him, he'd look you in the eye and listen to every word like it's the most important thing he's heard all day. Maybe even when he was busy, he'd somehow make time to help you with a math problem or with your golf swing. Maybe your idea of the perfect father is someone who would guide you to make good decisions, who would hold you tight when you're upset. Maybe he would know you so well, he'd understand when you weren't doing your best, but instead of getting mad or frustrated with you, he'd help you fix your mistakes and nudge you to say you're sorry when you've messed up.

This is how God loves you. He'll always listen. He'll always help. He'll always guide you. He'll always comfort you. And God will challenge you to be the best version of yourself, the best version of the person he created you to be. He is the perfect father. And he loves you.

~~~~~~~~~~~~~~~~~~

Write a letter to God, thanking him for being a good and perfect father. Feel free to mention specific ways he's been there for you, or specific ways you'd like to turn to him and trust in him in the future.

For I was hungry and you gave me something to eat, I was thirsty and you gave me something to drink, I was a stranger and you invited me in, I needed clothes and you clothed me, I was sick and you looked after me, I was in prison and you came to visit me.

—Matthew 25:35-36

Your days are busy with schoolwork, chores, and activities. Plus, you probably like to play, read, and visit with family and friends. But how much time do you take to help others?

If you're good with little kids, you could volunteer in your church's nursery or Vacation Bible School. If you're great at reading, you could tutor a younger student at your school or read books out loud to the kindergarten class. You could coach one of the younger teams or go through your closet and make a stack of toys you no longer play with to give to someone who needs them. Are you amazing at piano? You could give free lessons to someone who's interested in learning more about music.

Every gift you have comes from God. He gives you these gifts 1.) Because he loves you and 2.) So you can spread his love to others. Why not start spreading his love today?

Make a list of talents you could share to help someone out and/or things you could give away to help someone in need. Research ways to get started—organizations that could use your helping hands or old belongings. Your church or school is a great place to start. You can make a difference.

I was pushed back and about to fall, but the LORD helped me. The LORD is my strength and my defense; he has become my salvation.
—Psalm 118:13-14

Have you ever tripped in front of someone you were hoping to impress and felt super embarrassed? Is there something you do at home—a funny voice or a silly dance—that if your family mentioned to your friends you would turn red in the face? Have you ever given the completely wrong answer when the teacher called on you?

Embarrassing moments happen. But if you remember that Jesus has your back, you can let these uncomfortable moments go. See, Jesus isn't ever judging you. He loves you, and he thinks your funny voices and silly dances are hilarious.

Impressing others isn't the most important thing. Jesus is. When you let this truth really sink in, then you can shake it off, get back up, apologize fully confident that God will pick you back up and love you no matter what.

~~~~~~~~~

Draw an embarrassing moment. Now draw Jesus next to you. If you dropped your tray in the cafeteria, draw Jesus squatting next to you, helping clean up your mess with a speech bubble that says, "That's okay. It's no big deal. Everyone spills sometimes." Thank him for having your back. For being your strength and salvation.

My sheep listen to my voice; I know them, and they follow me. I give them eternal life, and they shall never perish; no one will snatch them out of my hand.

—John 10:27-28

Sheep react to their shepherd's voice. Another person can say the same words, the same phrases, in the same language as their shepherd, and the sheep won't respond. Why? Because sheep know their shepherd personally, and they trust him. They know he will lead them to fresh grass to eat. They know their shepherd will chase off wolves and keep them safe. He's there for them time and time again. So they learn to recognize his distinct voice—to trust him.

Jesus called himself the Good Shepherd because he has our best interests in mind. He'll keep us safe and guide us where we need to go. Listen for his voice, so when he calls, you'll know which way to go. When he's warning you, you'll be able to avoid trouble.

The more time you spend with Jesus the more you'll recognize his voice. The more you talk to him, tell him what's on your mind, what's bugging you, what you're excited about, who it's hard to be nice to, the more you'll get familiar with his voice. Talk to him today.

~~~~~~~~~~

Chat with Jesus. Don't know where to start? Thank him for something great or share something that was rough. Sit quietly and let him respond. You might feel warm or safe or relieved. You might think of something to do or someone to hug. The more you talk with him, the easier it is to hear him.

Each of you should use whatever gift you have received to serve others, as faithful stewards of God's grace in its various forms.

—1 Peter 4:10

What are you good at? Do you know God enabled you to be good at that thing?

You might practice your instrument for hours on end, but God gave you that love of music, put you in a home or school where someone encouraged you to play, made it affordable for you to get lessons and have access to an instrument. So play for him.

What does that mean? It means not groaning when you have to practice, but instead considering it a privilege that God gave you this gift. It means playing "Happy Birthday" for your dad's birthday, volunteering to play at a nursing home, or helping a younger sibling learn how to read music.

Are you awesome on horseback? God gave you a love for riding and financial resources to be able to take lessons and access a horse. He also placed you near some stables. Ride for him. Teach a younger rider how to put on a saddle. Talk about God and his love to other riders.

Whatever it is you're great at, God made you that way.

What is it you're good at? Write it down, then list some ways you could use that gift to glorify God this week—teaching someone else this skill, sharing about God with others on your team, etc. Try to do as many of them as you can.

King Solomon was greater in riches and wisdom than all the other kings of the earth. All the kings of the earth sought audience with Solomon to hear the wisdom God had put in his heart.

—2 Chronicles 9:22-23

It is hard to be wise. You can have all As in school and not have wisdom, because wisdom requires having experience and then taking that experience and applying it to your life to make good decisions.

You can read about riding a bike, listen to your friends talk about riding their bikes, but still get on the seat and not be sure what to do. You need to have the experience of pedaling, of shifting your weight from foot to foot, of moving the handlebars to steer, to truly have the wisdom needed to ride a bike.

It's the same way with life. You need to spend time with God to have the wisdom needed to navigate life. Praise God when things go well. Ask him for forgiveness when you mess up. Ask his advice when making decisions. Read the Bible. Go to church and/or youth group.

The more you experience God, the more wisdom you'll have about him. You'll be able to apply what you know about God to make good decisions and to live a full and happy life.

~~~~~~~~~~

Solomon was one of the wisest guys there ever was. He was packed full of God's wisdom. He wrote the book of Proverbs to share what God had taught him. Read Proverbs 1 today to gain more wisdom about God.

Many waters cannot quench love; rivers cannot sweep it away. If one were to give all the wealth of one's house for love, it would be utterly scorned.

—Song of Solomon 8:7

God's love for you is so huge. Even if you wanted to, you couldn't outrun God's love. You couldn't jump higher than it or outthink it. A tornado couldn't blow God's love away from you. The strongest football player couldn't pull God's love away from you. The richest man in the world couldn't pay God to stop loving you.

This also means no evil rumor can take God's love from you. No nasty social media post can stop God from loving you. No snide comment. No backstabbing frenemy could ever convince God to stop loving you. Nothing and no one could make him stop loving you, because he created you, and because you are his.

~~~~~~~~~~~~

Make yourself a Valentine from God, reminding you how incredibly much he loves you. Put it somewhere you'll see it all the time—the inside cover of your notebook, on your closet door, or in your sock drawer. Each time you see it, thank God for loving you. Don't forget to tell him you love him too.

But he said to me, "My grace is sufficient for you, for my power is made perfect in weakness." Therefore I will boast all the more gladly about my weaknesses, so that Christ's power may rest on me.

–2 Corinthians 12:9

Everyone has things they're *not* good at. And that's okay. It's a great reminder that the things you *are* good at are gifts from God, and that he's able to step in and help when you're struggling.

If you always drop the ball, but one day you catch it, this is your chance to give God the glory by saying, "God must have wanted me to catch this one."

If you struggle in grammar but finally bring home a perfect paper, thank God for helping you study and understand this concept.

If there's a bully who always makes fun of what everyone brings in their lunchboxes ask God to give you the strength to stand up and say, "People like different foods, and that's okay." When someone asks how you got the courage, tell them God gave you the strength.

You can't do everything well all the time. No one can. So when things do go well, give God the credit.

Can you think of something you're not great at, but God has helped you with in the past? Thank him for being there for you. Now, think of something you are great at. Make sure to give God credit for that too!

Peter and the other apostles replied: "We must obey God rather than human beings!"

—Acts 5:29

When your friends send each other pictures of their homework, that's cheating. When your teammates cut corners on the laps they're running, that's cheating. When your sister says, "Mom and Dad are out, they'll never know we watched this movie or ate this much ice cream," that's lying. When you have a secret social media account or delete a text so your parents won't see it, that's lying.

It doesn't matter if the problem is hard or your legs are tired or the rule seems silly. It doesn't matter if everyone else is doing it. You know right from wrong, and God calls you to be honest. Live for him, and he will reward you over and over again.

~~~~~~~~~~

How would you act if you knew God was watching you all of the time? What would you change? He is watching, but not like a spy—like someone who loves you and wants the best for you. Know that God's ways are always best and ask him for strength and faith to follow him no matter what others do.

Then Joseph said to his brothers, "Come close to me." When they had done so, he said, "I am your brother Joseph, the one you sold into Egypt! And now, do not be distressed and do not be angry with yourselves for selling me here, because it was to save lives that God sent me ahead of you."

—Genesis 45:4-5

Ever had a bad day? Felt like it was the end of the world? Weren't sure how you were going to move forward? Things might seem hopeless right now, but God is with you. He will use this time for good. He will get you through.

Joseph's brothers sold him into slavery. He was taken to a foreign country where he didn't know anyone and couldn't speak the language. Things don't get much worse than that! But God used this to move Joseph to Egypt, so Joseph could eventually work in the Egyptian government to save people from dying during a hard time.

If God can do that with a bunch of mean brothers, he can use whatever's going on in your life that seems rotten and unsolvable to make something good happen too. God will give you what you need for today, and then use where you are as part of his big beautiful plan for good.

What seems hopeless today? Write out these words: "Don't be stressed. Don't be angry. God will use this for good." Now say those words out loud in a prayer, "Dear God, please help me keep from worrying or being mad. Please give me faith that you'll use this problem for good. Thank you. Amen."

"On the day when I act," says the LORD Almighty, "they will be my treasured possession."

–*Malachi 3:17*

Have you ever caught snowflakes and marveled at their different beautiful patterns? Have you ever collected seashells at the beach and delighted in how each one has a special shape and a unique design? How about picked up leaves in the fall and thought how lovely the lemon yellow of one is and how pretty the ruby red of another is?

This is how God sees each one of us. He created each person so uniquely, with special patterns, lines, colors, shapes, and designs. He made you and everyone else with purpose, *on purpose*, to look exactly like you do.

And just like all snowflakes are spectacular and every shell is precious and each leaf is stunning, each person is a treasured possession to God. This includes you. He is blown away by the beautiful shades of your skin, hair, and eyes. He is amazed by the shape of your nose and loves the patterns of how your mind learns and the designs of how your heart feels.

To him, you are a treasured possession.

Depending on the time of year and where you live, go outside and observe something beautiful in nature—birds, pebbles, or the eyes of people you know. Notice how each is unique, but each is also beautiful. Thank God for creating you how he did, for making you his treasure.

Then you will call on me and come and pray to me, and I will listen to you. You will seek me and find me when you seek me with all your heart.

—Jeremiah 29:12-13

You probably go a lot of different places. Some of them you might look forward to going to. Some of them you might dread.

When you go to a new place, do you look around, figure out where the bathroom is, where the doors are, the best place to sit down, or maybe where the snacks are? Do you look for God there?

Because God is everywhere. He is every single place you go. And God says when you seek him, you'll find him. When you talk to him, he'll listen. That's pretty cool. So when you're in your fun and favorite spots, thank him for all the things that make them grand. And, when you're in unknown or unpleasant places, make sure you look for God so he can bring you a smile, some rest, or some peace. When you look for him, God is everywhere.

~~~~~~~~~~~~~~~~~~

As you go different places over the next few days, think about God being there. Look for him. He might show himself as a hug, a laugh, a familiar face in a sea of strangers, or a calm breeze when you're feeling stressed. He wants you to find him. Reach out and feel his love.

Do not fear, for I have redeemed you; I have summoned you by name; you are mine. When you pass through the waters, I will be with you; and when you pass through the rivers, they will not sweep over you. When you walk through the fire, you will not be burned; the flames will not set you ablaze.

—Isaiah 43:1-2

There are things you will go through that will feel lonely, that will feel scary, that will feel sad. Maybe you've gone through some of these things already—maybe you're going through one of these things right now.

When you feel like the very worst is happening, God is with you. He will not let you down. He will not leave your side. Over 100 times the Bible says, "Do not fear!" But sometimes life can be stressful or cause you to worry. How will you escape anxious thoughts and find calmness?

You'll do it by believing God when he says he will be with you. You'll do it by reminding yourself of these truths again and again, until you feel them down deep and understand how fully God loves you.

If there is something you're frightened about, write down a sentence saying, "_____ (fill in the blank with your worry) can't harm me." Put the note somewhere you'll see it the next time you're feeling scared.

But you will receive power when the Holy Spirit comes on you; and you will be my witnesses in Jerusalem, and in all Judea and Samaria, and to the ends of the earth."

–Acts 1:8

When was the last time you told somebody about Jesus? Have you *ever* told anybody about Jesus? The last thing Jesus did before going up to heaven was ask the disciples to tell the world about him. It might feel a little awkward to you, or maybe you're just not quite sure what to say, but you can talk about Jesus just like you talk about anything else that matters in your life.

If someone asks you what you did over the weekend, you can tell them about your volleyball game, the movie you watched, *and* what you learned in church. If someone you know broke their arm or is sad their dog is sick, you can tell them you're praying for them. The more you talk about Jesus, the easier it gets. And if Jesus is important in your life—the most important thing in your life—doesn't it make sense to talk about him?

Write down someone's name who you will talk to Jesus about today or tomorrow. Maybe you can tell a friend about this devotional you're reading, or use Jesus in a story or poem you write at school. Ask God to give you the right words and the courage to share about him.

For the grace of God has appeared that offers salvation to all people. It teaches us to say "No" to ungodliness and worldly passions, and to live self-controlled, upright and godly lives in this present age.

–Titus 2:11-12

Grace is the free gift of love from God. Grace means God knows everything you've ever succeeded and failed at and thinks you're awesome anyway. It means God's heard you sing, seen you dance, knows how many books you've read, and no matter how well you did or didn't do any of those things, God thinks you're amazing. God loves you so completely you don't have to prove anything to him. You don't have to have the last word, have the teacher call on you, pass the blame, brag about accomplishments, or score the most points.

None of those things change God's love for you. This frees you to be the best version of yourself. To say no to things you know *aren't* right and to stand up for things you know *are* right. To not obsess over the things you have or want, knowing nothing you own makes you more or less valuable to God. He already thinks you're fabulous!

~~~~~~~~

What tempts you? Boasting about the things you've seen or done? Joining in when everyone at your lunch table gossips? When you're tempted, get in the habit of reminding yourself that God loves you. It will remind you how special you are and that you never have to prove yourself to him or anyone else.

In a large house there are articles not only of gold and silver, but also of wood and clay; some are for special purposes and some for common use. Those who cleanse themselves from the latter will be instruments for special purposes, made holy, useful to the Master and prepared to do any good work.

—2 Timothy 2:20-21

Have you ever cleaned out your closet? Were you amazed at how much stuff you ended up giving or throwing away or at how much more space you had after sorting through everything?

Just like closets accumulate stuff, your life accumulates stuff too. From time to time, it's good to clean up your life and sort through what's in there. You might have to give up a habit you've outgrown. You might have to toss some things you've worn out. And you might have some things you should have never put in your life in the first place.

When you clean out your life, you get rid of things that distract you from God and make room for all of his love and all of the awesome things he has in store for you.

Is there anything in your life you need to clean out? Write it down on a scrap of paper. Talk to God about how you'd like to get rid of it. Ask for his help and guidance. Now, rip up the scrap and throw it in the trash as a reminder of how you're going to clean up your life.

"Is not this the kind of fasting I have chosen: to loose the chains of injustice and untie the cords of the yoke, to set the oppressed free—and break every yoke? Is it not to share your food with the hungry and to provide the poor wanderer with shelter—when you see the naked, to clothe them, and not to turn away from your own flesh and blood?"

–Isaiah 58:6-7

It's hard to imagine that so many girls your age literally don't have a place to sleep or food to eat. But it's true. And that means:

1. You can be grateful for all God has given you.
2. You can help God's children who aren't so fortunate.

Volunteering is the perfect way to do both of the above. There are so many ways you can help. Talk to a parent, teacher, or pastor to get ideas of how you can make a difference. Some ideas are collecting cans for a food pantry, volunteering with your youth group, or writing letters to people who need a friend. And there are so many more! When you help others in need, you are reminded of how fortunate you are, *and* you share God's love with others. Double blessing!

Talk to an adult about some ways you can help people in need. Make a list and then pick one you like. Plan how you will help someone less fortunate.

Now it is God who makes both us and you stand firm in Christ. He anointed us, set his seal of ownership on us, and put his Spirit in our hearts as a deposit, guaranteeing what is to come.

–2 Corinthians 1:21-22

The first thing a teacher usually asks you to do when she passes out a piece of paper is to write your name on it. The moment you write your name on that paper it increases in value. By writing your name on that test, painting, or worksheet, you become responsible for what's on that paper and what happens to it. You'll put effort into whatever goes on that paper, because you could be evaluated, graded, or put into a group based on what you do with it.

God puts his name on you.

He put the Holy Spirit within you. The moment God did this, you immediately went up in value. God is concerned about what happens to you. He puts time and energy into helping make you the best you can be. Knowing God's name is on you means he gives you an A+, puts you in his group of favorites, and loves you forever.

What have you written your name on that you feel particularly proud of? A sketch? An essay? Think of what you'd do to keep it safe, how much time you put into it. Thank God for wanting to care for you so deeply that he wrote his name on you.

If any of you lacks wisdom, you should ask God, who gives generously to all without finding fault, and it will be given to you.

–James 1:5

Should you babysit for the neighbor or go to your best friend's house to watch a movie? Should you go to the ball game with your dad or stay home and work on the big history project that's due Monday? Should you quit Girl Scouts? Join book club? Start your own club?

There is only so much time in a day, and there are so many great opportunities for you to use your twenty-four hours. But God has a purpose for you, and knowing that purpose helps you make good use of the gift of time. Start there. Ask yourself, "Does babysitting or visiting a friend best fit with God's plans for me?" It depends. How badly do you need the money? Is your friend going through a tough time? Sometimes the answer is clear. If the answer isn't obvious, then just start talking to God about it. You don't need special words or phrases; just talk to God like you'd talk to a friend. He will help you solve your problems and make your decisions. He loves it when you come to him for advice.

What advice do you need today? What choices will you have to make? Write one or two down. Next, ask yourself how these things do or don't fit in with God's purpose for you. Now, talk to God about them. Sit still and allow him to help you sort out the solutions.

126

> But if serving the LORD seems undesirable to you, then choose for yourselves this day whom you will serve, whether the gods your ancestors served beyond the Euphrates, or the gods of the Amorites, in whose land you are living. But as for me and my household, we will serve the LORD."
>
> *—Joshua 24:15*

How you act and spend your time points to what is most important to you. After a long day of school do you come home and grump at your little brother or give him a hug? After you lose a game do you gripe about the ref or encourage your team to keep their chins up? When you have some extra time do you always do something for yourself? Or do you look to see how you might make someone else smile?

Being a Christian means choosing to follow God all the time, even if you're tired or stressed or discouraged. It means acting and thinking in a way that makes God happy. Would someone who sits next to you in class or who plays against you in softball know that God is important to you? Would your family? Today, ask yourself if your actions show the world that you have chosen to follow the Lord—that Jesus is what you value most.

~~~~~~~~

Think about your typical day—who do you talk to, what's your attitude, how do you react to good and bad events? Can people tell you're a Christian by your actions? If not, ask God to help you live for him, so those around you will know you choose the Lord.

The LORD said, "Go out and stand on the mountain in the presence of the LORD, for the LORD is about to pass by." Then a great and powerful wind tore the mountains apart and shattered the rocks before the LORD, but the LORD was not in the wind. After the wind there was an earthquake, but the LORD was not in the earthquake. After the earthquake came a fire, but the LORD was not in the fire. And after the fire came a gentle whisper.

–1 Kings 19:11-12

God is so huge and powerful. He's the guy who created giant mountains and endless oceans. But that doesn't mean God always comes to us loud and large and bright.

Sometimes God gives you a whiff of fresh grass that reminds you springtime is coming. Sometimes you reach into your pocket and find the exact amount of change to buy yourself and a friend a cupcake. Sometimes a kid in the hall smiles or your sister hugs you just when you need it the most. All of these gifts are sweet ways God is with you. Be on the lookout for his gentle, loving whispers to you today.

Think back through the past 24 hours and jot down some of the small, sweet whispers of love God has given you—an unexpected card in the mail, your favorite meal for dinner, etc. Thank God for all of the little (and big) ways he loves you.

*For to us a child is born, to us a son is given,
and the government will be on his shoulders.
And he will be called Wonderful Counselor,
Mighty God, Everlasting Father, Prince of Peace.*
—Isaiah 9:6

Who do you go to when you have a problem? Your best friend? A parent? A sibling? A teacher? Sometimes when problems are too jumbled for you to figure out on your own, someone might suggest talking to a counselor. A counselor is someone who's trained to guide you through problems—social problems, emotional problems, and personal problems. It could be a school counselor, a counselor from church, or a counselor in an office.

Jesus is not called any old counselor, but Wonderful Counselor. He is the best listener, gives the best advice, is always available to you, and always knows exactly what you need. Read the Bible—his living word. Talk to him about everything. He's never afraid to tell and show you difficult things, but he'll never share with you something that isn't true or right or just. He'll keep all your secrets. They're safe with him.

~~~~~~~~~

What's something you don't know if you could ever tell anyone? Tell it to Jesus right now. He already knows all about it and how it makes you feel, but he also knows how to make it better. Trust him and his teachings. He'll never let you down.

He got up, rebuked the wind and said to the waves, "Quiet! Be still!" Then the wind died down and it was completely calm.

–Mark 4:39

You might face real-life storms like being pounded by snow or whipped by wind or shaken by crashing thunder. Storms can be unsettling or even scary. But you can find peace during those storms. Jesus said, "Quiet! Be still!" and the wind stopped. Since he can do that, he can certainly keep you safe—even when the power goes out.

But there are other kinds of storms too. Someone you love might get sick or have to go to the hospital. No matter how hard you try, you might still struggle with something at school. Adults might argue. Someone may pick on you or hurt your feelings.

Jesus can calm these storms too. He can give you strength and wisdom and endurance to get through tough times. Trust in his power, and ask for him to give you a hand. He'll help you feel completely calm.

Write out the verse above. When you're frightened, reread this verse, reminding yourself of what Jesus has the power to do. Then start praying. Tell Jesus you know he can calm storms. Ask him to calm the flip-flopping in your stomach and to keep you safe.

And if you greet only your own people, what are you doing more than others? Do not even pagans do that?

—Matthew 5:47

God expects you to be kind to everybody he made. And since he created everyone, that means you're supposed to try to be nice to *all* of them—even the people who drive you crazy. Even the people who never seem to notice you. Even the girl who's the ball hog or the teacher's pet or the class gossip. That doesn't mean asking them all to your sleepover, but it does mean waving. It means making room for them at lunch or the assembly. It means being kind whenever possible.

Why? Because that's how you'd want to be treated. Because that's how God treats *you*. To God, you always matter. Help someone else feel that way today.

Was there a time recently when you saw someone you knew and didn't greet them? Replay that incident in your mind and think through what you could have said or done to make that person feel valuable. Decide to say hello to and smile at someone you normally wouldn't today.

But for you who revere my name, the sun of righteousness will rise with healing in its rays. And you will go out and frolic like well-fed calves.

—Malachi 4:2

When your coach says, "Another set," or your teacher says, "We're going to have a test tomorrow," or your grandma says, "I need you to unload the dishwasher before you go to bed," it can sometimes feel like too much. You might feel like you cannot do it, like you've already used everything you had and you don't have anything left.

But God says, "Yes, you can."

God promises sunshine and a fresh new day ahead of you. God promises rest and healing and re-energizing to start all over again. How do you get that rest, healing, and energy? By praising him and asking him for the little extra you need. It's that easy. Turn to Jesus for a little turbo boost when you need it most today.

~~~~~~~~

Copy the above verse and put it somewhere you'll see when you're overwhelmed or tired. If you struggle waking up, put it on your alarm clock. If you're exhausted when you get home from school, tape it to the hook where you hang your backpack. Ask God for some of that extra energy right now.

The LORD will fight for you; you need only to be still.

—*Exodus 14:14*

Remember all of the stories where the hero comes in and saves the day? When Charlotte the spider writes empowering messages in her web to save Wilbur the pig? When Anna jumps in front of the sword to save her sister, Elsa? When the mice labor up the stairs with a heavy key twice their size to unlock the door and free Cinderella?

Have you ever wondered who will fight for you? When someone makes fun of you? When someone hurts you and you don't have the words to speak up or shout out? When you feel trapped or in danger or like there's no way out?

God will. God will stand in front of the sword, unlock the door, and remind you how wonderfully made you truly are. In fact, he's not just fighting for you; he's fighting for all of his people. No matter what you're up against today, God is on your side. He will fight for you and the good of his kingdom. You can count on him to rescue you from evil.

Sketch a picture of (or write about) your favorite hero saving the day. While creating your drawing, tell God all about something you might need him to save you from. Tell him how you feel and how you're stuck. Then ask him to be your hero.

Set your minds on things above, not on earthly things.

—Colossians 3:2

Do you collect anything? Coins? Lotions? Fuzzy socks? Books? Pillows? It's fun to find a new item for your collection, to line it up with the others, to show your friends or post on social media.

There's nothing wrong with enjoying the sweet fragrances, soft textures, great stories, and cool treasures of the world. But there is a problem when *things* become too important. When they define you. When you think for even a moment that what you *have* has anything to do with who you *are*.

Because your value rests in the fact that you are loved by Jesus. To God you smell lovely, the story of you is fascinating, your patterns and designs are beautiful. He wants to be near you and to spend time with you, because God treasures you. Focus on God's great love for you today.

List or draw something you collect. What's the newest addition to your collection? What item would you like to add next? Each time you look at or use the items in your collection thank God for loving you, for choosing you, for thinking of you as his treasure.

Cast all your anxiety on him because he cares for you.

–1 Peter 5:7

If you have a test tomorrow and fractions seem inside out and upside down, you might feel stressed. You might get anxious when you're running behind for practice, knowing the coach makes the whole team do push-ups if someone is late. If you left your lunch on the bus you might worry about what you'll eat.

But how does it feel when someone in your family takes time to help you with your homework? When you actually get to practice before your coach? When the teacher brings pizza to reward the class? That's how God wants to make you feel all of the time. He may not step in to solve all your problems for you, but he will help you through whatever makes you anxious—giving you peace and providing you comfort. God loves you and wants to take your worries from you.

Hand over to him anything that worries you today.

Is there something that repeatedly causes you anxiety? Draw or imagine a well, a bucket, and the things that stress you out peeking out from the bucket. Label the well "God." Now, draw everything in the bucket being dumped down the well. Imagine the splash as God takes your worries from you.

Forgive us our sins, for we also forgive everyone who sins against us.

–Luke 11:4

Anne Frank was a Jewish girl who lived in Amsterdam during World War II. At that time, the German Nazi army was instructed to arrest Jewish people and take them to concentration camps. Anne and her family hid from the Nazis for two years. During that time, she kept a diary.

Since soldiers would destroy Anne and her family if they were found, she had to stay indoors in a small space with seven other people, live on little food, and only speak or move around at night so they wouldn't be caught. Anne could have been angry at the Germans, hateful towards them for what they were putting her and her family through, but in her diary she wrote that even though her life felt bleak, she still believed people were essentially good.

If Anne can find people good at heart, then it is possible for you to find something good in the people around you—even the seemingly annoying and mean ones. If you ask him, Jesus forgives you for everything you've ever done wrong. Try finding something good about everyone else today.

Who drives you crazy? Think of something good about them. Have you seen them pick something up for somebody, talk to the new kid, or do a good job on their report? Ask God to help you see them through his eyes—to see the good in them.

*As for those who were held in high esteem—
whatever they were makes no difference to me;
God does not show favoritism.*

–Galatians 2:6

The rich and famous have something about them that makes you notice, that makes you comment, that might even make you a little jealous, or wish you had more of "that," whatever that is.

But you are already perfect. Exactly how God created you. It's awesome to have huge dreams. If you get excited acting in the local theatre program and want to continue acting, then striving to one day receive an Academy Award is fantastic! But you don't need to win any awards to get God's attention. You've already got it.

God made you with so many special gifts. They're all in there just waiting to be put to use. You are beautiful, strong, capable, and talented. No matter what anyone else looks like or achieves, God loves you. And he always will.

~~~~~~~~

If there is anything you don't love about yourself, talk to Jesus about it right now. Ask him to help you see yourself through his eyes—all of your talents and beauty, all the things that make you special and awesome. Ask him to help you believe it all the way down to your toes. You are beautiful.

"For I know the plans I have for you," declares
the LORD, *"plans to prosper you and not to harm
you, plans to give you hope and a future."*
—Jeremiah 29:11

What is that dream in your heart? That dream to use your musical gifts to write worship music, to teach in inner-city schools, or maybe to become president and make changes that impact millions of lives?

At the very moment you were born God started equipping you to do great things for him. He created you for a very specific purpose that nobody else could achieve, that nobody else is capable of doing. He gives you all the tools you need to achieve those dreams whether that's writing the next great novel or discovering the cure for a disease.

Even when people tell you you're too short, too tall, too young, or not good enough, God knows better. Don't let anyone stomp on the dreams God has put in your heart. Instead, set your mind on achieving the great things he has planned for you.

If you could do anything in the world what would it be? Make a list of three things you can do this week to help launch that dream. It could be researching a topic at the library, running sprints, watching how-to videos, or emailing someone who does this thing. Start chasing God's dream for you today.

Therefore encourage one another and build each other up, just as in fact you are doing.

–1 Thessalonians 5:11

Just like God has plans for you, he has plans for everyone else you meet. What if you could be the person to help someone else achieve their dreams?

That airplane made out of Legos your little brother built? Take time to look at it, to listen to his explanations of the wings and landing gear. Who knows? He might go on to design a solar-powered jet someday. That new cookie recipe your mom made that looks suspicious? Taste it. It might become your new favorite treat, or she might use that recipe to win a contest. That music video your best friend has been talking about recording? Ask her to rehearse in front of you. Give her advice and cheer her on.

Only God knows what our futures hold, but you can have an active part in making someone's day. Your kind words can help someone else believe in themselves and in the plans God has for them.

~~~~~~

Choose someone you can encourage today. Decide how you will inspire them—write them a note, send them a text, draw them a picture, give them a hug or a compliment—and then do it!

I urge you to live a life worthy of the calling you have received. Be completely humble and gentle; be patient, bearing with one another in love.

–Ephesians 4:1-2

Friendships can be tricky. One friend might get mad at another. Someone might say something mean about someone else. A girl you usually eat lunch with might start eating lunch with another group. Each situation will be different, but God gives you instructions on how to handle all the drama:

1. Be humble. Don't worry about being important, noticed, or right all the time. Take time to listen to others and consider their viewpoints.
2. Be gentle. Take a breath before you shout out a comeback, a defense, an insult, or point the blame.
3. Be patient. Trust that God is at work in all of the simmering and in-between moments.
4. Love. Show love to the friend who is hurt and the friend who supposedly hurt her. Show love to the girls who stayed at your table and to the one who left. By letting everyone know they're uniquely awesome, they'll be able to find the courage and kindness to resolve the problems.

Get out your markers and make some word art out of the following words: Humble, Patient, Gentle, and Love. As you doodle, ask God to help you be all of these things to both your friends and your frenemies.

I know your deeds, that you are neither cold nor hot. I wish you were either one or the other! So, because you are lukewarm—neither hot nor cold—I am about to spit you out of my mouth.
—Revelation 3:15-16

Have you ever left a bottle of water in the car in the hot summer sun? You get back in the car from running around outside—hot, sweaty, very thirsty—and grab your water. You take a sip, and . . . Ew! It's warm. Not refreshing at all.

Or have you set a cocoa down at your place, gone back later, and wrapped your hands around the mug hoping for warmth only to find it the same temperature as the room? Then you take a sip and it doesn't warm you up inside at all? So disappointing!

God has made you to be awesome! He's given you ideas and talents and he wants you to use them full-on for him. He doesn't want you sitting still, letting your cool ideas get warm or the plans you're all heated up about cool down. Be energized today and live to the fullest!

Think through your week ahead and how you can live it fully. Do you have a test? Make sure you study. Are you visiting with family? Put down your phone or book and spend time in conversations. Going on a field trip? Keep your eyes open for new discoveries.

Sow your seed in the morning, and at evening let your hands not be idle, for you do not know which will succeed, whether this or that, or whether both will do equally well.

–Ecclesiastes 11:6

So many opportunities await you! Countless flyers come home from school about different teams, sports, and trips. Your church might offer mission trips, retreats, festivals, and game nights. Your community might host parades, contests, and races.

You certainly don't have time to try ALL of them, but you do have the chance to try something new.

If your teacher announces an essay contest about a topic that interests you, why not write down your thoughts? If there's a pie-baking competition for the Fourth of July festivities and you enjoy cooking, this is your chance to try a pie. Never played football before? Why not sign up with some friends for the flag football league at the park?

God has loaded you with abilities—some of them you haven't even discovered yet. Try something new today, and see what you can do!

What are some things you've never done before but would like to try? Write them down in your journal, talk to God about which ones he might like you to check out, and circle one you can attempt this month. Invite a friend to join you.

Let us not become weary in doing good, for at the proper time we will reap a harvest if we do not give up.

–Galatians 6:9

It's challenging not to join in when your friends gripe about the grumpy girl at school. It can be exhausting to smile at your brother every time he picks on you. It can seem worthless to study every week for your spelling test, when week after week you don't do as well as you hoped.

But God sees your every effort. Every single time you strive to do what is noble and right he notices. And God will use your kindness, patience, and endurance for good. Your friends might rethink how they look at that girl. Or that girl might rethink how she looks at herself. Your brother might pick on you less or his teasing might bother you less. You might just ace one of those spelling tests or you might be developing fantastic study skills that will help you in the long run.

And even if the results aren't that obvious today, your determination will pay off. God will make great things happen when you don't give up.

Ask God for some help to stick with doing the right thing. Imagine each time you choose well you're watering a flower, and although you can't see it growing immediately, each drop of water helps it eventually bloom.

143

Blessed is she who has believed that the Lord would fulfill his promises to her!

–Luke 1:45

You are loved.
God has plans for you.
You are treasured.
God will never leave you.
You are forgiven.
God will return for you.
You are beautiful.
God will protect you.

These are just a few of God's promises. On any given day they may be easy to believe or difficult to get your mind around. But no matter what your mood, your circumstance, the weather, how you're feeling, or what your schedule looks like, these promises are still true.

God created you. And when the creator of the universe took time out to make you, he did it specifically and intentionally. He will protect, love, and care for his beautiful creation always—that's you!

Write out each of the promises listed above. Use different colors. Make the ones that are most important to you bigger, bolder, fancier. Tape these promises on your mirror. Read them each morning reminding yourself they are true.

Out of his fullness we have all received grace in place of grace already given.

—John 1:16

You know those free samples at the grocery? Someone hands you a toothpick with a brownie bite or a chunk of cheese on the end. You don't have to pay for it. You just get to eat it. And when you walk to a different aisle someone else might hand you another treat to try—a chip dipped in salsa or a sip of a new juice. You don't have to cut or pour it. You don't even have to order or ask for it. It's all prepared and waiting for you.

That's what God's grace is like. He hands you new flavors down every aisle of life. You don't have to work for his love or forgiveness. You don't have to beg or reach way up high or eat your lima beans first. Yes, God wants you to love others, be honest and choose wisely, but he doesn't *make* you do anything to earn his free samples of grace. He gives them to you first. And he hopes that you enjoy the delicious flavor of his love so much, you'll want to share it with others.

Do you have a certain store or place in a store where you get free samples? What's so great about them? Think of a "sample" of love or forgiveness God has put in your path recently. Thank him for it. Now ask him to keep your eyes open for all the surprises he sets out for you.

I keep my eyes always on the LORD. With him at my right hand, I will not be shaken.

–*Psalm 16:8*

Have you ever shaken up a soda and then opened it? What happened? Foam and fizz probably exploded everywhere!

That same thing can happen when you allow yourself to get shaken up. When your coach criticizes you, when your parents ask you to clean up your sister's mess, when you can't find your shoes, how do you handle it? Do you get flustered and fussy and let your anger or emotions explode everywhere? Or do you keep your eyes on Jesus?

When you look to Jesus, he will remind you to stay calm. He loves you no matter what your coach says, what your sister does, or where you left your shoes. The next time you find yourself about to explode, take a deep breath, and think of what Jesus would want you to do.

What shakes you up and makes you feel like exploding? Talk to Jesus about it right now. Tell him when it upsets you, how it upsets you, why it upsets you, who upsets you, and ask him for peace. Imagine the opposite of bubbles, maybe a smooth milkshake, and imagine sipping it the next time you feel shaken.

For he chose us in him before the creation of the world to be holy and blameless in his sight. In love he predestined us for adoption to sonship through Jesus Christ, in accordance with his pleasure and will.

—Ephesians 1:4-5

Want extra salsa or mayo? Just request it. Not a fan of lettuce? Not a problem, just ask for no lettuce. When you go through the line at a choose-your-own-ingredients type restaurant like Subway or Chipotle it can be so much fun. You can get all your favorite flavors, the ones you crave, the ones that make you happy, in the combinations you like best. No matter how your friends or family order, your meal is still exactly how you hoped it would be.

Just like you choose no cheese or extra chicken because that's what brings you the most pleasure, God chose you because you make him happy. He intentionally and specifically chose you because he loves you and to him you are exactly who he wanted.

~~~~~~~~~

Just like you build your own sandwich, God picked every ingredient that went into making you. Thank God for purposefully building you exactly how he did and for thinking you are wonderful.

So then, brothers and sisters, stand firm and hold fast to the teachings we passed on to you, whether by word of mouth or by letter.

–2 Thessalonians 2:15

On a super windy day, leaves dance across the road. Branches might snap off trees. Litter can blow out of trashcans, and sometimes the garbage can itself blows over! These things can't hold on. They don't have arms, hands, or fingers to grip onto their home.

On a super stormy day of your life, it might feel like the wind is blowing everything around. Unkind words might breeze right out of friends' and family members' mouths. Insults, hurt feelings, frustration, and tension might be flying around every which way. It might seem like you can't manage anything, like everything's out of control.

But there is good news. You do have arms, hands, and fingers to cling to the most secure base there is—Jesus. He is so strong, true, right, just, and loving that there is nothing as solid as him to hang onto.

~~~~~~~~~~

Find something sturdy—a railing, a desk—and wrap your hands around it. Now talk to Jesus about anything blowing around in your life. As you hold your steady base, imagine it is Jesus, solid and strong. Let his strength fill you. The next time you're feeling overwhelmed, do this again remembering Jesus will hold you in place.

His divine power has given us everything we need for a godly life through our knowledge of him who called us by his own glory and goodness.

–2 Peter 1:3

Have you ever tried to bake cookies, only to find you only have one egg, not two in the fridge? Or tried to put together a building set, but found they didn't put one of the pieces you needed in the box? Maybe a teacher explains, "Since you already know how to multiply fractions, it should be easy to divide them." And you think to yourself, *Yikes, what if I **don't** know how to multiply fractions?*

Some days you might feel like you're missing some of the pieces you need to move ahead, but God gives you everything you need. He already knows who you'll need to meet and when you'll need to meet them. God knows where you'll need to go, how you'll need to get there, and how much the ticket will cost. God might not give you the airfare or the A, but he'll give you time to study, someone who will explain it to you, and a way to earn the money you'll need. No matter what dream God has planted in your heart, he will provide all the tools you need to achieve his plans for you.

Bake something today. Not handy in the kitchen? Make a sandwich or a bowl of cereal. As you pull each item out, consider all the different things you need to make this food. Thank God for all of the ways he provides for you, the ways he gives you what you need.

Dear friend, do not imitate what is evil but what is good. Anyone who does what is good is from God.

–3 John 1:11

There is always "that girl" in class, on the team, or in the club. She cuts others down and everyone laughs. She posts nasty-grams on social media and everyone likes them. She shows up in a pair of shorts and for some reason everyone thinks they're cool, even though they're not that interesting or different. Everyone thinks she is something special, and she'll be the first one to tell you all about it.

When you stop to think about her appeal you can't figure out why everyone is so charmed by her. But they are. Be careful here.

Even if this girl is getting all the attention, it is not the kind of focus you really want. When you stop to think about who you truly want to be, I'm guessing it's not nasty or snarky or self-important. She is not worth imitating. No one is. Remember, God sees you as his masterpiece. He made you wonderfully to inspire awe. You don't have to earn attention at anyone's expense. You don't ever need to be like anyone else. You are already prized by the King of Kings.

List some things you know God created you to be. Stuck? Here are some ideas—fast, good listener, clever, full of energy. Focus on being these things today. When you're tempted to imitate someone else, go back to your list, and remember all of the great things you already are.

But by the grace of God I am what I am, and his grace to me was not without effect.

–1 Corinthians 15:10

Everyone has labels attached to them. There's the tallest boy in class and the kid who has the really short, funky hair at youth group. There's the star of the field hockey team, the girl with the gorgeous voice, the family with the giant van, and the smartest kid in math.

You have some labels attached to you too—maybe you're short or tall or redheaded or brunette. You might have the label of what sport or instrument you play or which neighborhood you live in or if you ride a car or bus to school.

And although those labels may partially describe who you are—yes, you're the girl with the Golden Retriever—none of those labels actually define you. Your ultimate label is that you are a child of God. And that means you are loved, you have value, and you are important.

Look at some labels in your clothes. Design your own labels describing God's love for you. They could say beautiful or courageous or anything else that makes sense to you. Attach them to some of your stuff, so when you see the labels, you'll be reminded of who you are.

*Whatever you do, work at it with all your heart,
as working for the Lord, not for human masters.*
—Colossians 3:23

Wiping off the table, memorizing your math facts, dusting the family room, writing definitions, unloading the dishwasher—some things feel more like work than fun.

But some work needs to be done to enjoy the fun. Studying helps you do better in school, which will eventually help you get the job you're dreaming about. Cleaning the house keeps away germs and bugs and gives you nicer space to study and play in.

It's all in how you look at it. Don't gripe about the teacher who assigned the paper you have to write. Instead, consider it a chance to work on your handwriting or learn something new. Don't grump at your mom for asking you to feed the cat. Instead, thank God for your cute kitty.

Whatever is on your to-do list today, stop thinking about it as a chore, and start thinking of how God might use it as an opportunity for good.

What tasks do you most dread—folding your clothes, rewriting spelling words? Think of how you can relook at those things that need to get done. How might God be using them for good? How can you use them for good?

Jesus answered, "I am the way and the truth and the life. No one comes to the Father except through me."

—John 14:6

You need a password to log into your account at school, to check the weather on your phone, and to purchase a new song. You might have a combination to get into your locker or to open your garage at your home. If you forget the password or combination, it can be so frustrating! When you can't get in where you want to go, when you're locked out you feel blocked, stopped in your tracks.

But Jesus can open all doors. Whatever Jesus has planned for you, whatever Jesus hopes for you, he will not only give you the code, he is the code. He is the way to God. Nothing you're supposed to do or achieve for God is locked or blocked from you. You may still forget your password from time to time, but know that Jesus will always let you in, help you get closer to God, and get you where you're supposed to go for him.

Change one (or all) of your passwords to something that will remind you of Jesus and his love for you. That could be the letters or numbers signifying a favorite Bible verse or the letters Jesus with your favorite number before and after. Be creative. Every time you enter your password you'll be reminded how Jesus unlocks life for you.

The wise woman builds her house, but with her own hands the foolish one tears hers down.

–Proverbs 14:1

Have you ever built a Jenga tower, a Lego set, or a gingerbread house? There is something so satisfying about building up the walls, making it steady, and watching it grow right before your eyes. There is planning involved, thinking through the steps—where to build it, how to make the base stable, how to make the pieces connect, and what you want it to look like when you're finished.

Your life can be just like that. If you decide to build your life on the steady base of Jesus, you're already off to a great start. As you go, you'll need to think through next steps. How can you make the things you do today matter for tomorrow? Will this be something that helps you grow or makes you wobbly? What parts are important for you to include in your life?

Take action today. Get building a beautiful life for yourself—one full of hope, faith and love—and know that you aren't in this construction project alone. With God at your side, you can build something amazing!

Grab some blocks and build a tower. While you're constructing it, consider what you'd like your life to look like someday. As you add blocks to your structure, talk to God about what you can be doing today to build a great life with him.

He said: "The LORD is my rock, my fortress and my deliverer; my God is my rock, in whom I take refuge."

–2 Samuel 22:2-3

You measure how hard minerals are with a system called the Mohs scale. The hardest mineral is a diamond. It is a ten out of ten on the Mohs scale. It is so hard that the only thing that can cut a diamond is another diamond!

Why is it important to know how hard a rock is? Because the harder the rock, the more it resists scratching. The hardest rocks can make it through storms, travel great distances, endure intense heat, and they're the best at polishing other rocks.

The Lord is your rock—the hardest kind of all, stronger than a diamond, higher than a ten on the Mohs scale! Why is that important? Because it means God can help polish you into the best version of yourself. God can protect you from being scratched. God can help you through the storms of life, travel great distances with you, and help you stand strong no matter how much heat you're in.

God is the ultimate rock. Cling to his strength today!

Go outside and gather some small rocks. Try scratching them against each other. Whichever one is the strongest will make the most marks on the others and have the fewest on it. Put the strongest rock in your pocket or backpack as a reminder of God's strength in your life.

> Yet I will rejoice in the LORD, I will be joyful in God my Savior.
>
> —*Habakkuk 3:18*

Today you can choose. You can choose to complain about how tired you are and how gross those vegetables taste and how everything is so unfair.

Or you can be amazed by everything God has created, by everything he does for you, and for all of the great things he places in your path day after day. You can wake up and thank God that you live in a country where girls can go to school and learn, where girls can grow up to become anything they want to be. You can thank God for your coziest pair of sweats and for the softness of your puppy's ears. You can find joy in getting to watch your favorite show or the chance to see a new one.

God's gifts are all around you. Are you looking for them?

Write down anything that made you grumble in the last 24 hours. Next to each thing you listed, write down two things you've experienced in the last 24 hours that brought you joy. Thank God for all of the ways he blesses you.

Now what I am commanding you today is not too difficult for you or beyond your reach.

–Deuteronomy 30:11

You might not be able to reach the cereal box on the top shelf of the store, the chocolate chips that are high up in the cupboard, or that itchy spot in the middle of your back, but you can reach everything God has in store for you!

Not sure if you're brave enough to say your lines loud enough in the play? God will give you courage to speak up. Having a hard time not snapping at your sister when she's bossy? God will give you the self-control to stay quiet and turn away. Uncertain if you'll ever be able to earn enough money to go on the youth trip? God will help you think up some creative ways to raise funds.

Whatever God is asking you to do; he will be like a step-stool enabling you to get to everything you need.

Make a list of things you'd like to do. It can be anything from training a service dog to making a new friend to staying focused on your homework, so you can do your best. Reach both hands high into the air, and imagine God giving you a boost to reach everything he has in store for you.

*The Lord will rescue me from every evil attack
and will bring me safely to his heavenly kingdom.
To him be glory for ever and ever. Amen.*

—2 Timothy 4:18

There are loads of reality shows in which people try to stay safe in the middle of scary circumstances. There are shows about fishermen in stormy seas, people interacting closely with wild animals, and others racing their way through risky obstacle courses while staying in one piece. These shows feel dangerous, but time after time the boat makes it through the storm, the crocodile doesn't bite, and even though someone topples, they only end up with a bump. On TV there's always a rescue crew just out of the camera's view ready to save the day.

You can stay away from the treacherous sea, poisonous snakes, and slippery steppingstones by avoiding signing up for a reality show. You can also stay away from the dangers of this world by hanging out with Jesus. He is your rescue crew waiting to save your day. When something frightens you, God can comfort you. When you feel under attack, God's got your back. When you feel like you're slipping, God will steady you. Just ask him.

What frightens you? Imagine yourself maneuvering through this danger like you're on a reality TV show. Every time it looks like you'll slip, get stung, or fall overboard, God miraculously steps in and saves the day. Thank Jesus for always protecting you and ask him for help in any reality you're worried about today.

Therefore, if anyone is in Christ, the new creation has come: The old has gone, the new is here!

–2 Corinthians 5:17

If you make a sandcastle, but it leans too far to one side, you can knock it down and start all over again. You'll still use the same sand, but you can shape it better, rework it, learn from your mistakes in making the last one, to build a sturdier, better version.

When you start following Jesus, you also get a chance to start over. Any of the bad habits or thoughts you had before can go away. Jesus smashes them down so they're not even there anymore. And then Jesus uses your original grains of sand and reforms you into the most spectacular sandcastle on the beach. Jesus will make you a stronger, more joyful, more lovely and loving version of yourself.

~~~~~~~~~~

If you have a sandbox or live near a beach, make a sandcastle. If not, make a quick sketch of one. Notice what you'd like to fix or make better, then smash it or grab a fresh sheet of paper. Rebuild or redraw an even better castle. Imagine Jesus shaping and sketching you into your best form.

> Let us acknowledge the LORD; let us press on to acknowledge him. As surely as the sun rises, he will appear; he will come to us like the winter rains, like the spring rains that water the earth.
>
> *—Hosea 6:3*

Bad days:

You looked through all of your drawers and your favorite pair of jeans isn't there. You open the fridge to grab a snack and find somebody ate all the yogurt. You turn on the TV, but your favorite show isn't on. Practice got cancelled because of the rain.

Good days:

You get a brand new pair of jeans. Your mom makes homemade cookies just because. Your favorite show is having a marathon. You won the championship game.

Sometimes things you depend on let you down. Other days you get unexpected surprises. But God is good all the time. You can always depend on him. Just like the sun rises every morning, God will be with you each and every morning. He'll be there on the days when everything seems to go wrong and when everything seems to go right. With God, your day can always be better.

List some things you depend on—like the bus picking you up for school or your grandma sending you birthday cards. Think about how great it is to count on them. Thank God for always being there—every day, every way, for being the one who will never let you down.

My son, if sinful men entice you, do not give in to them. If they say, "Come along with us" . . . my son, do not go along with them, do not set foot on their paths.

—Proverbs 1:10-11,15

Lemmings are small rodents whose habitat is grasslands or the tundra, like you'd find in Canada or Alaska. There is a myth that if one lemming runs to the edge of a cliff and jumps, all the other lemmings will foolishly follow. Tons of people believe that lemmings are the ultimate example of falling for peer pressure. But even lemmings are smarter than that. And so are you.

Just because some girls have boyfriends or some girls wear super short shorts doesn't mean you have to or should. Just because some of your friends didn't do their homework or talk back to their parents doesn't mean you should follow suit.

You know who you are. You are a child of God. You were made intentionally by God for a specific purpose. Don't let what anyone else does today influence your decisions or lead you off the amazing path God has laid out for you.

Google lemmings. Read both the made-up legends and the truths about them. Thank God for giving you the ability to make your own decisions and act upon them. Ask Jesus to help you make the best choices and the wisest decisions.

He says, "Be still, and know that I am God."
–Psalm 46:10

Hurry up. Get moving. Do you have everything? What time is it? Hop in the car. The bus will be here any minute. We're going to be late!

Does this sound like your life at all? There's schoolwork and chores and friends and family. You are involved in sports, volunteering, music, or dance. The list goes on and on and your calendar gets more and more full.

God says, "Be still." When was the last time you were completely still? Sleeping doesn't count. When you're still, you can exhale some of the stress. When you're still, you have a chance to talk to God, and even better, hear him talking to you. When you're still, great ideas come to you and problems work themselves out in your head.

Before you go off in another direction take a moment to be still.

~~~~~~~~~~~~~~~~~

Find a quiet spot. Turn off all your electronics. Put down your pen. Close your eyes. Thank God for being so amazing. Sit in silence for a few minutes thinking about the peace and love God offers.

For everyone who asks receives; the one who seeks finds; and to the one who knocks, the door will be opened.

—Matthew 7:8

Have you read the stories in which someone discovers a genie and is granted three wishes? In the stories, the person often wishes for foolish things, and all of a sudden they're left with something silly or nothing at all.

What if you had three wishes? What would they be? Real wishes. Not just, "I wish it would stop raining," or, "I wish I didn't have to finish my homework," because then you'd end up like the silly main character of the story with a wasted wish. Eventually it will stop raining. And you probably need to do your homework, so you'll have the knowledge necessary to chase the dreams God has put in your heart.

Jesus says that if we ask him, if we look for him, if we knock on his door, he will answer us, show us what we're looking for, and unlock the door. How awesome is that? The only catch? You have to ask, look, and knock. Have you asked Jesus, through prayer, to help make your wishes come true? Have you looked in Scripture for answers to your questions? Have you knocked by stepping forward and believing he can do it? Why not start now?

Write down three wishes. Take some time to really think them through. Ask Jesus for help in making these wishes come true. Keep asking and listening. He will unlock the door to your dreams.

163

We have this hope as an anchor for the soul, firm and secure.

–Hebrews 6:19

Storms and powerful currents can push and tug huge, sturdy boats off course and take them somewhere they were never supposed to go. But sailors can use anchors to provide stability and stop their boats from drifting.

Everybody drifts in her faith from time to time. You might plan on being patient with your sister, but you end up saying something horrible when you're tired. You might want to trust God, but something impossible is going on and it's hard to believe everything will turn out okay. You might want to include the unpopular girl, but you're afraid your friends will laugh.

Jesus is your anchor. He can hold you in place and keep the storms and currents of life from blowing you around. Just like a sailor has to decide to use their anchor for it to work, you have to decide to rely on Jesus to keep you from drifting. When things feel out of control, call out to Jesus. He will steady you and keep you safe and secure.

Draw an anchor and put it somewhere you need to be reminded of how Jesus will keep you safe, will keep you from drifting even in the biggest storms. Maybe draw it on the bottom of your shoe, so you can look at it while you're at rehearsal, or on the cover of your notebook, so you can see it in class.

Being confident of this, that he who began a good work in you will carry it on to completion until the day of Christ Jesus.

—Philippians 1:6

You might be the first girl in your family to go to college, or you might start an orphanage for girls in another country. You might be the one who invites classmates to start praying before school or who gets teammates praying before games. You might beat the record for being the leading all-time international soccer scorer or maybe you'll even invent a car that uses less energy.

Whatever that awesome thing is God started in you when he made you, he will make sure it happens.

Today you might feel discouraged. You might not have any idea what God has in store for you. You might not think you're all that awesome or capable. But God knows better. He sees all of your potential because he gave it to you. He knows what awesome things await because he's planned them for you. And he knows that no matter how you feel right now, he will make sure the good and special thing he has designed for you to do will happen.

Draw a line. Mark points at the beginning, middle, and end of the line. Label the first point, "God began a good work in me." Label the second point, "God is carrying out a good work in me." Label the last point, "God will complete the good work."

So do not throw away your confidence; it will be richly rewarded.

–Hebrews 10:35

Is there anyone you see or talk to on a regular basis that makes you feel small, dumb, weak, or awkward? Maybe it's the way they speak to you or treat you that makes you walk away with doubts about yourself. Maybe they are smarter or faster or bigger than you, but that doesn't make them better.

Jesus always sees you as awesome! He made you. He loves you. He doesn't want you to ever have to worry about what someone else thinks about you. You never have to doubt your ideas, your thoughts, your way of doing things, because Jesus is the one who made you exactly how you are. You never have to wonder why you're not as _____ as someone else, because you're not supposed to be like them.

Confidently celebrate each and every unique part of you that Jesus made you to be.

An acrostic poem is a poem in which the first letter of each line together spell out a word or phrase. An acrostic for "snow" might be:

> **S**parkling
> **N**umb fingers are worth it
> **O**utside adventures
> **W**onderland of ice

Write an acrostic for your name—make each letter of your name stand for something amazing about you.

All Scripture is God-breathed and is useful for teaching, rebuking, correcting and training in righteousness, so that the servant of God may be thoroughly equipped for every good work.
—2 Timothy 3:16-17

You've probably needed to check out some sort of instruction packet or website. Schools have expectations about attendance and homework. Sports have rules so players and referees all know and agree about what does and doesn't count.

When it comes to life advice, the Bible is your ultimate resource. It's like Google, but way better. Have a question about how you're supposed to act when your parents are driving you crazy? It's in there (Exodus 20:12). Wondering if it's such a good idea to wear that T-shirt? It's in there (Proverbs 31:25). Doubting yourself? The Bible will remind you who you are (Psalms 139:14). Unsure what to do next? The Bible will remind you God will guide your steps (Matthew 6:33).

The more you read the Bible, the better equipped you'll be to face your day, to face your life. Read it today.

Pick a devotion from this book that has impacted you. Look up the verse at the top of that day in the Bible. Read the paragraph or chapter that verse is in. It will give you even more context as to what that verse might be talking about and will help those encouraging words stick in your mind and heart.

Therefore, I urge you, brothers and sisters, in view of God's mercy, to offer your bodies as a living sacrifice, holy and pleasing to God—this is your true and proper worship.

–Romans 12:1

Your body might be tall, short, thin, wide, curvy, or angular. You might have big feet, long fingers, or eyelashes that go on and on

Since God spent so much time making you, it's important for you to take care of your body. Eat fruits and vegetables daily to get the vitamins your body needs to work. Vitamin C in strawberries and oranges helps you fight off germs. Vitamin A in sweet potatoes and carrots helps your sight. Drink milk to make your bones strong. Exercise to keep your muscles moving and your heart beating full force. You can jump rope in the garage or on the playground. And after all of that playing and running and jumping, make sure you get enough sleep.

Take care of the amazing body God created especially for you!

~~~~~~~~~

Make a chart with four columns:
- fruits and veggies you eat
- each glass of milk you drink
- exercising
- getting at least seven hours of sleep.

Give yourself a sticker or draw a smile each time you do something good for you.

But the Lord is faithful, and he will strengthen you and protect you from the evil one.

–2 Thessalonians 3:3

Sometimes the littlest thing can throw you off course. Someone borrows your brush without asking. Your teacher tells you to be quiet, even though you weren't talking. You can't get the website to load. You can just feel the frustration building up inside of you—fists clenching, teeth gritting. It seems like everything is going wrong or everyone is against you.

But everyone isn't against you. God is on your side. He is faithful. He will never leave you. Even when it seems like everything is a mess, he will strengthen and protect you.

Take a deep breath. Take another. You can get through this. Maybe all you need is to ask someone for a hand to find something that's lost, solve a problem, or turn off your computer, restart, and try again. God is faithful. He cares about every detail of your life, so he won't leave you in the midst of the little things. You can get through this and all obstacles with his strength and protection.

How did you act the last time you were irritated? Did you slam a door, stomp your foot, or storm off by yourself? Did you pray? The best thing to do when you're frustrated is to talk to God. Talk to him now about something annoying and allow his peace to fill you.

Don't let anyone look down on you because you are young, but set an example for the believers in speech, in conduct, in love, in faith and in purity.

–1 Timothy 4:12

When the Taliban took control of her valley in Pakistan and took away her right to attend school, eleven-year old Malala started a blog speaking up about how important education is for girls. As a result of her blog, many news outlets interviewed Malala. The *New York Times* even made a documentary about her. Her story and hard work helped lead to the First Right to Education Bill in Pakistan. She went on to be the youngest person ever (at age 17) to win the Nobel Peace Prize. By using her voice to speak up, this young girl made a huge difference to many girls across the world.

Somebody might need to hear your voice today. There might be someone you encounter who needs to be encouraged, who needs to know they have the ability to make good choices, or who needs to know there is a God who loves them.

You have a voice. Use it today to spread love and light.

What's important to you? It could be helping an animal shelter find homes for abandoned animals or standing up for the first grader who's always picked on. It could be as simple, but important, as smiling at everyone. You can make a difference. Find at least one way to stand up for what you believe in today.

But one thing I do: Forgetting what is behind and straining toward what is ahead, I press on toward the goal to win the prize for which God has called me heavenward in Christ Jesus.

—*Philippians 3:13-14*

Yesterday might have been a bad day. You might have made a mistake, gotten in an argument, or felt ready to give up on a goal. But that was yesterday.

Today is a brand-new day. God has huge plans for you, and he will give you the energy, the resources, and the ability to achieve them. Today is the best day ever to launch yourself forward, straight into those awesome plans.

If you were too tired yesterday, start again today well-rested. If you couldn't figure something out yesterday, research it today—see if there's a YouTube video explaining it or ask someone for help. If you were nervous yesterday, ask God for some courage today. If someone was unkind to you yesterday, forgive her today.

Today you can run and rush forward to your goals, your dreams, and an amazing future.

What dream has God planted in your heart? Draw or envision yourself crossing a finish line. That finish line symbolizes you achieving your dream. What can you do today to press on toward it?

And let us consider how we may spur one another on toward love and good deeds, not giving up meeting together, as some are in the habit of doing, but encouraging one another—and all the more as you see the Day approaching.

–Hebrews 10:24-25

There are tons of reasons you could come up with to skip youth group or Bible study—you like to sleep in, you're shy, you're outgoing but none of your best friends go there, you'd really like some time to relax. Fine.

But the truth is, it's really good for your soul to hang out with other Christians. That doesn't have to be 24/7, but all the things we've talked about in this devotional—about making good choices, about being kind even when it's hard, about tapping into God's strength and courage, about trusting in God and his promises—all those things are a whole lot easier to remember and to hold onto when you hang out with other people who believe the same things.

So, even if they're not your group of closest friends, make a conscious effort to connect with some Christians this week. They'll cheer you on and encourage you to be the best you can be.

When does your youth group meet? Don't have one? Ask your parents to look into whether there's a Christian group for girls your age nearby. Talk to God about the excuses you have to not go, then ask him to take those away. Give it try.

For this is what the Sovereign LORD says:
I myself will search for my sheep and look
after them.

—Ezekiel 34:11

What about the days when you feel like you're at the end of your rope? When you are too tired to get up? Too defeated to try again. What about the days when you've prayed and prayed and it doesn't seem like things are getting better, when you're not sure where God is or how you could possibly go about finding him?

Don't worry. God will find *you.*

Just like if you lose your dog, you'd walk around, drive around, call around, yelling his name, putting up signs until you find him—God will do the same for you. It doesn't matter if you ran away from God, or if you got distracted and roamed down the wrong path, or if you're plain lost. God will search for you. And when he finds you, God doesn't ever want to punish you, he just wants to take care of you and love you.

Have you ever felt distant from God? Sometimes you might feel that way, but God is never far from you. Reach out and touch the nearest thing to you. That's how close God is. Keep your hand on that thing and thank God for always being within reach.

For we know, brothers and sisters loved by God,
that he has chosen you.

–1 Thessalonians 1:4

The student with the best essay will be chosen for a scholarship. The girl who makes the best poster promoting the event at the library wins a stack of books. The person whose number they pull out of a hat wins a gift card to your favorite ice cream shop. They're announcing the name, posting the grand prizewinner, and pulling out that number. You hope it's you!

You know what? God chooses you every time. It's *your* number he pulls out of the hat, *your* name he reads out loud, *you're* the special individual he wants to reward. It doesn't matter how many other people have entered or how talented or smart or rich or fast or tall they seem. It doesn't matter if you've never won anything before in your life. You have won God's love.

Close your eyes and imagine one of the scenes from above, and the winner is being announced. Picture God saying *your* name out loud, saying, "I choose you. I love you!"

I pray that the eyes of your heart may be enlightened in order that you may know the hope to which he has called you, the riches of his glorious inheritance in his holy people.

—*Ephesians 1:18*

Have you ever looked at your house from the back or from across the street and noticed something you'd never seen before? Maybe you've moved your bed from one corner of your room to another and everything seems a little different, newer, more interesting, even though it's your same room.

Today you probably see your life as just that—a day in your life. You'll wake up in your home, get dressed in your clothes, do your chores, study, go to your activities with the people you know. What if you took a different view? What if you stepped back and intentionally looked at your life from a different angle, from the perspective of all the things God has in store for you, all the little chances he's giving you. God is sprinkling love, protection, and opportunities throughout your day today. Sometimes it just requires getting a different view. Open your eyes to the brightness.

Ask your parents if there is a piece of furniture or a step stool you're allowed to stand on. Look around a familiar room from this different perch. What looks better? Why? Now take a different view of your life and be amazed at all the hope and love God has scattered throughout it.

Shout for joy to the LORD, all the earth. Worship the LORD with gladness; come before him with joyful songs.

–Psalm 100:1-2

Cheerleaders shake their pompoms and shout when their team scores. Coaches jump up and down on the sidelines when a player scores. Audiences clap after a great performance. Cats purr when you scratch their favorite spot under their chin. Friends who haven't seen each other in a while squeal with delight when they catch sight of one another.

Do you ever thank God out loud for all the wonderful things he does for you? This can mean singing out loud to worship music or hymns in church. This can mean praying out loud by yourself or for your family before a meal or bed. It could mean walking to the mailbox and seeing a gorgeous spring flower and simply saying, "Thank you, God, for making that and letting me see it!"

Silent prayers and conversations in your head are fantastic. God loves to talk to you however and whenever you want. But every now and then, get excited about how much God loves you and shout your praise out loud.

Thank God out loud for something that makes you happy. If you're nervous, do it somewhere no one will hear you. God won't mind. But thank God out loud for something you've seen or enjoyed today. Get in the habit of finding something that brings you joy each day and praising God out loud for it.

My goal is that they may be encouraged in heart and united in love, so that they may have the full riches of complete understanding, in order that they may know the mystery of God, namely, Christ, in whom are hidden all the treasures of wisdom and knowledge.

–Colossians 2:2-3

What would you do if you found a million dollars and didn't have to give it back? It's fun to dream about finding a secret treasure. You've probably seen a movie or read a book in which the hero finds gold and jewels or the detective discovers where the thief has hidden the money.

But if you know Jesus, you *have* found treasure and you never have to give it back. It's not something you can use to buy the coolest clothes. It won't get you on television. It's better. You see, the riches of Jesus are understanding who you are and how specifically you're loved. You are a daughter of the one true King. That makes you a real live princess. Not in a silly sappy way, but in a really cool way, in the way that means you are treated as special, respected, and appreciated.

The treasure of knowing Jesus is knowing that he rolls out the red carpet for you. That he will give you courage and strength and help you choose wisely, because he loves you.

What are you doing with the treasure of knowing Jesus? Are you sharing his love with others? Finding joy in each day? Looking for new opportunities to use your gifts for him? How can you use the riches God gives you today?

Gracious words are a honeycomb, sweet to the soul and healing to the bones.

—Proverbs 16:24

Bullying usually begins with one person using unkind words about someone else. The words might seem harmless. They might sound normal. Just a comment like, "Let's sit over here," except *here* means away from a specific person. Or whispering a secret to a friend in front of another girl, so she can't hear. It might be a general statement about how you can't believe some people have never read that book. But in all of those instances somebody is intentionally excluding someone else. Somebody is implying they are better than someone else. Those words are powerful.

Unkind words are powerful, but kind words are just as powerful. A kind word can change everything. Saying, "Let's sit *with* these people," or "You don't need to whisper, everyone can hear." or "I think everybody reads and likes different books" are all quick phrases that totally change the mood from possibly hurting someone's feelings to possibly making them feel better.

Think over your words today. Choose to speak sweet, healing words.

~~~~~~~~~~~~

Look up the definition and then some synonyms for the word, "include." Think over what the word means. Talk to God about ways you can use kind words today to make others feel included. Thank God for always including you in his love, his grace, and his protection.

178

"And I myself will be a wall of fire around it," declares the Lord, "and I will be its glory within."

—Zechariah 2:5

A lot of different things are going to come your way today. Are you ready?

People will compliment you, ask you to do things, expect you to have done things, and criticize something you've done. You will soar, and you will stumble. You will have a moment when you wish you had more, and you will have a moment you are so thankful you have what you have.

Through each and every one of these instances, God is with you. He will protect you like armor, like a wall of fire, from insults and injuries. He will motivate you from within to keep going and stay true to who he made you to be. God keeps you safe from the outside and builds you up from the inside. No matter what comes your way, God has you covered.

Draw a picture or write a poem about how God covers you like bubble wrap, keeping you safe from harm, and how he fills you like a protein bar, giving you energy and strength. As you create, ask him to help you realize how fully he is with you in all you do.

Cast your cares on the LORD and he will sustain you; he will never let the righteous be shaken.

–Psalm 55:22

When the teacher calls you out into the hall. When you hear a friend whispering about another friend. When you have to get up in front of everybody. These things can make you sweat, your throat feel tight or your heart beat fast. Worries, stresses, and anxieties in life are unavoidable. But you get to control what you do with them.

God says, "Give them to me." And just like you can ask your dad if he'll help you carry your heavy backpack, or your sibling to help you carry your laundry basket upstairs, you can ask God to help carry the things that concern you. All of a sudden everything is lighter, simpler to manage. Hand over your worries to God today and breathe a little easier, knowing you've got the strongest helper ever to help carry your load.

Create a "worry box." Find a small cardboard box and some scraps of paper. Every time you get stressed or worried this week, write it down on one of the scraps and put it in the box. As you do so, tell God you don't want this worry anymore. You are handing it over to him.

180

Come near to God and he will come near to you.
—James 4:8

You know where to find your friends. You might see them at school, at your lessons, or at the park. You know where to find your family—you most likely live under the same roof! If you want to get close to your dog all you have to do is call for her, and she'll come running. But how do you find God?

The cool thing about God is he's everywhere. Attending church, going to youth group, and reading your Bible are awesome places to find God. But just like you can find your friends other places than the steps of school, you can find God other places too. You can find reminders of him everywhere you go. You can consider God's warmth as you cozy up to a bonfire, marvel at his majesty as you gaze at the glow of a sunset, be reminded of his constancy in the beat of a drum, and sense how much he loves you when you hug your grandma (knowing God created Grandma and her love for you too).

All you have to do is look for him, talk to him, thank him for his awesomeness, and he will be there.

~~~~~~~~~~

Even though this book is ending, God's love for you will never end. He is everywhere, and he is always with you. Make a list of all the places you'll go tomorrow. Write down how you might find God there. Thank God for being everywhere!